2/98

HOW
PROUDLY
THEY WAVE

HOW PROUDLY THEY WAVE

Flags of the Fifty States

Rita D. Haban

Lerner Publications Company ■ Minneapolis

All words printed in **bold** are explained in the glossary

Cover photo courtesy of the State of Alabama, Bureau of Tourism and Travel

Flag artwork by the Flag Research Center, Winchester, Massachusetts 01890
Updated flag artwork by Darren Erickson, pp. 26, 64, 90.

The colors of flags and flag reproductions may vary slightly from time to time.
This can result from the age and condition of the flag or from different dye lots,
printing processes, fabrics, and/or paper.

Copyright © 1989 by Lerner Publications Company
Third printing 1995 contains updated information.

Library of Congress Cataloging-in-Publication Data

Haban, Rita D.
  How proudly they wave: flags of the fifty states/by
Rita Haban.
     p. cm.
  Includes index.
  Summary: Describes the history and significance of each
state flag.
  ISBN 0-8225-1799-X (lib. bdg.)
  1. Flags—United States—States—History—Juvenile literature.
[l. Flags—United States—History] I.Title. CR113.2.H33   1989
929.9'2—dcl9   89-2302
                                              CIP
                                              AC

Manufactured in the United States of America
3   4   5   6   7   –   JR   –   99   98   97   96   95

CONTENTS

ACKNOWLEDGMENTS

Special thanks must be given to Helene F. Fox, O.H.C., former principal and teacher of elementary schools, for her observant work with the rough draft; to Mary Eckart, the flag lady, who manufactures all types of flags and who enthusiastically hand-carried my work to the Flag Congress of San Francisco for evaluation in 1987; to George Cahill, member of NAVA, the North American Vexillological Association, for all his constructive suggestions; and to Whitney Smith, Ph.D., executive director of the Flag Research Center.

It is with deep appreciation that I express my gratitude to the following individuals and organizations. I am particularly grateful for the time, effort, and cooperation they extended so readily to aid me in my research and for the numerous items and historical information they have supplied.

All quotes are used with their written permission.

Thank you all, sincerely.

- Alabama State Department of Archives and History
- Stephen McAlpine, governor of Alabama
- Alabama Department of Commerce and Economic Development
- Alaska Division of Tourism, David W. Stewart
- Office of Lt. Governor, State of Alaska, Christina Kennedy, Secretary
- Arizona Library and Archives, Marguerite B. Cooley, Director
- Office of Arizona Secretary of State, Rose Mofford
- Former Governor of Arkansas, Orval E. Faubus
- Arkansas Secretary of State, W. J. "Bill" McCuen
- California Secretary of State, March Fong Eu
- State Historical Society of Colorado, Alice W. Wallace
- Connecticut Secretary of State, Julia T. Tashjian
- Delaware Development Office, Ricardo E. Allen
- Florida State Librarian, Dorothy Dodd
- Florida Secretary of State, George Firestone
- Georgia Secretary of State, J. Maxwell Cleland

- Office of Lt. Governor, State of Hawaii, John Waihee
- Idaho Historical Society
- llinois Secretary of State, Jim Edgar
- Illinois State Library, Head Reference Librarian, Kathryn M. Harris
- Indiana Secretary of State, Edwin J. Simcox
- Iowa State Department of History and Archives
- Iowa State Librarian, Linda L. Greene
- Former Kansas Secretary of State, Jack H. Brier
- Kentucky State Treasurer, Frances Jones Mills
- Kentucky Historical Society-Archives Museum Library, Frances Coleman, Librarian
- Louisiana State Archives and Records Commission, Wade O. Martin, Jr., Raymond H. Downs
- Louisiana State University Library, Evangeline Lynch, Librarian
- Maine Secretary of State, Rodney S. Quinn
- Maryland Department of General Services, Kenneth B. Webster
- Maryland Secretary of State, Lorraine Sheehan
- Massachusetts Secretary of State, Vincent R. Caroleo
- Former Governor of Massachusetts, John Volpe
- Michigan Historical Commission, Geneva Kebler, Archivist
- Michigan Secretary of State, Richard H. Austin
- Minnesota Historical Society, Michael Brook, Assistant Reference Librarian
- Department of Archives and History, State of Mississippi, Mrs. Lindsay Grimes, Archivist
- Missouri State Historical Society, Richard S. Brownlee, Director
- Historical Society of Montana, Michael Kennedy
- Montana Department of Commerce, Sherryl Pouliot
- Former Secretary of State, Frank Murray
- Nebraska Secretary of State, Allen J. Beermann
- Nebraska State Historical Society, Donald F. Danker, Archivist
- Nevada Historical Society, Clara S. Beatty, Director
- New Hampshire Historical Society
- Former Governor of New Hampshire, Wesley Powell
- New Jersey State Library Archives, Robert A. Hamm, Senior Librarian
- Museum of New Mexico, Division of History, Mrs. J. K. Shishkin, Research Librarian
- The University of the State of New York, State Education Department, Albert B. Corey, State Historian

- North Carolina Secretary of State, Thad Eure
- North Dakota Secretary of State, Ben Meier
- Ohio Secretary of State, Sherrod Brown
- Oklahoma Historical Society, Muriel H. Wright
- Oregon Historical Society, Barbara Elkins, Reference and Genealogy
- Former Governor of Pennsylvania, Roy A. Schafer
- Rhode Island Secretary of State, Susan L. Farmer
- Rhode Island Historical Society, Clarkson A. Collins III, Librarian
- South Carolina Secretary of State, John T. Campbell
- Former Governor of South Dakota, Archie Gubbend
- South Dakota Secretary of State, Alice Kundert
- Former Governor of Tennessee, Buford Ellington
- Tennessee Historical Society
- Texas State Library, James Day, Director of State Archives
- Utah State Historical Society
- Vermont Historical Society
- Vermont Secretary of State, James H. Douglas
- Virginia Historical Society, Virginius C. Hall, Jr., Curator of Rare Books
- Washington State Historical Society, Richard P. Hanson, Assistant Librarian
- West Virginia Historical Society, James L. Hupp, State Historian and Archivist
- Former Governor of Wisconsin, Anthony S. Earl
- State Historical Society of Wisconsin, Margaret Gleason, Reference Librarian
- Wyoming Secretary of State, Thyra Thomson

PREFACE

This work began when my children were in elementary school and one son was assigned to research the history of the state flag of Ohio.

It was such a difficult task to find this information that I wanted to make it easier for other students in the future.

However, times were troubled. We were in the midst of the explosive '60s. Our country continued through the turbulent '70s. The work was shelved.

Battered, we survived, emerging into the reasoning '80s. These are the years to take stock and forge ahead.

With this in mind, I have reworked the book, and I have also added the history of the flags.

I hope you will enjoy rediscovering America.

INTRODUCTION

Flags have different meanings for different people, but they are powerful symbols for everyone.

Our national flag has 50 white, five-pointed stars appearing on a dark blue **canton,** the top inside quarter of the flag. Each star represents one of the 50 states that make up the United States of America.

Each of these states has a flag of its own. Some state flags reinforce traditional values, and some express gratitude for gifts of the land and/or sea. Each flag tells its own story, and each individual history inspires a better appreciation of our country as a whole.

The dates that appear under the names of the states are the dates on which the state flags became official. Sometimes there is a difference between the date when a state legislature passes a law and the date when the law becomes official.

ALABAMA

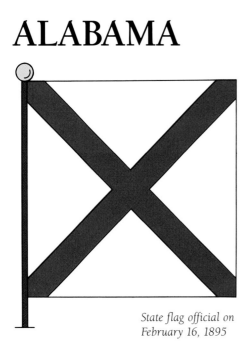

State flag official on
February 16, 1895

Alabama, whose motto is *We Dare Maintain Our Rights,* joined the Union in 1819.

As time passed, the citizens of the state felt great unrest about the question of slavery. Finally, during a session on January 11, 1861, the Alabama House of Representatives voted to secede from the Union. During the session, an enthusiastic, cheering crowd burst into the house chamber and unfurled a large flag made by ladies from Montgomery, Alabama. The new flag was run up the staff over the capitol, and a gun squad fired a salute.

One side of this unique blue flag pictured the goddess of liberty holding an unsheathed sword in her right hand. In her left hand, she held a small flag with a single star. Forming an arch above this figure were the words *Independent Now and Forever.*

There was a large cotton plant in full fruit and flower on the flag's reverse side. A rattlesnake lay at the roots, poised and ready to spring into action. The snake signified the danger of treading upon the rights of people. Beneath the plant were the words *Noli Me Tangere,* "Dare Not Touch Me."

The life of this flag was shortened because the flag was left flying one night during a gale. Someone forgot to take it down, and by morning the flag was torn and tattered. State officials lowered the ragged flag and placed it in the governor's office for safekeeping. It remained there until after the Civil War when it was taken by a group of Union soldiers called "Wilson's Raiders." Alabama's flag ended up in a museum cabinet in Des Moines, Iowa, where it remained until 1938, when it was returned to the state of Alabama. This flag is known as the Secession Flag of Alabama.

On March 4, 1861, while Alabama's own flag was folded away in the governor's office, the first Confederate flag was hoisted over the dome of the state capitol.

In 1861, the Confederate armies began to use the "battle flag" which was designed to be easily distinguished from the Stars and Stripes of the Union. The Confederate flag had a blue cross of St. Andrew (an X-shaped cross) with a white border against a red **field.** Thirteen stars dotted the blue cross.

When the dust of the Civil War had settled, Alabama rejoined the Union, but the state didn't have a flag. On February 16, 1895, a design that is still in use today was accepted. The flag is a red cross on a pure white field, a design that recalls the Confederate flag.

Alabamians are proud of their state flag. The people of the state helped pass a law that requires the state flag to be flown over the capitol when the legislature is in session. The flag must also be displayed beside the flag of the United States on school grounds when school is in session.

ALASKA

State flag official on
May 2, 1927
(Under the territory)

Vitus Bering, who led a Russian expedition, is credited with making the first recorded sighting of Alaska in 1741. Russians explored Alaska and made contact with the native Inuits and Aleuts as early as 1784. *Alaxsxaq* or *Alyeska* is the Aleut name for Alaska, which means "The Great Land."

The United States purchased the region from Russia in 1867 for a little more than $7 million. William Henry Seward, then secretary of state under President Abraham Lincoln, negotiated for the United States. Many Americans of that era didn't see the wisdom of the purchase, and they referred to Alaska as "Seward's Folly" or "Seward's Ice Box."

Alaska tried for many years to become one of the United States. But most Americans thought of the northern territory, which is as large as Texas, California, and Montana combined, as a cold, desolate place.

In time, Alaska became known for its mining camps and fisheries, its hides and lumber, its high rugged mountains, and its totem poles. These impressive poles, carved and painted by the Tlingit and Haida tribes, were often topped with the figure of a thunderbird or raven. Native American legend tells how the raven stole the sun, moon, and stars for the tribes to use.

Prospectors discovered gold in the Klondike in 1897, which marked the start of the gold rush. The precious metal hidden in the hills and rivers brought thousands of "sourdoughs," miners who survived mainly on a diet of sourdough bread. Other people followed to build towns and profit from the miners' newfound wealth.

In 1916, Alaska made its first request for statehood, but Congress refused to admit it as a state.

In 1926, Alaskan members of the American Legion decided that people in the United States needed to know more about Alaska if the northern territory was ever to be accepted into the Union. They held a contest in the public schools for the design of a territorial flag.

Benny Benson, an orphaned 13-year-old from the Jesse Lee Mission Home at Seward, Alaska, created the winning design. His sketch was accompanied by the following explanation:

> The blue is for the Alaskan sky and the forget-me-not, an
> Alaskan flower. The North Star is for the future state of Alaska,
> the most northerly of the Union. The Dipper is for the Great
> Bear—symbolizing strength. [Great Bear is another name for
> the constellation that includes the Big Dipper.]

Finally, on June 30, 1958, the Congress of the United States voted Alaska its statehood. The northernmost state has since proved to be more valuable than even Secretary Seward could have imagined. In 1968, a huge oil field was discovered at Prudhoe Bay. It is the largest oil field in North America.

Alaska was officially admitted into the Union by presidential proclamation on January 3, 1959, as the 49th state.

ARIZONA

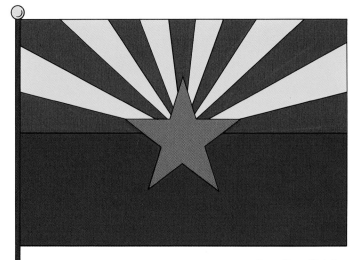

State flag official on
February 27, 1917

Arizona was part of the New Mexico Territory in 1846, but by 1863, Congress had voted to make Arizona a separate territory. Finally, on February 14, 1912, President Taft signed the statehood bill, making Arizona the 48th state to enter the Union.

The state flag of Arizona was designed by Colonel Charles W. Harris, adjutant general and chief administrative officer of Arizona. According to Colonel Harris, the suggestion for a state flag came from the 1910 Arizona rifle team. When team members attended the national rifle matches in Ohio, they noticed that all the other teams flew a distinctive flag. However, the Arizona team was without an emblem of any kind. Colonel Harris immediately began to work on the problem.

When designing the flag, Harris considered both historical values and colors. Blue and yellow were Arizona's colors; red and yellow were the colors carried by the Spanish conquistadors when they entered Arizona in 1540.

Harris designed a flag with a blue **field,** the same blue as that in the United States flag. Since Arizona was the largest producer of copper in the nation, a copper-colored, five-pointed star was put or **charged** in the center of the flag. Harris also thought that the rays of the setting sun would be appropriate for the flag of sunny Arizona, so in the upper half of the flag, red and gold rays, the old Spanish colors, spread from the star to the edges of the flag.

Some members of the state legislature that adopted this flag didn't like its design, however, and a number of votes were cast in opposition. The governor gave silent expression to a similar feeling. Rather than signing or vetoing the bill, he permitted the act of adoption to become law by waiting the required period of time for it to become effective. The flag was adopted on February 27, 1917.

ARKANSAS

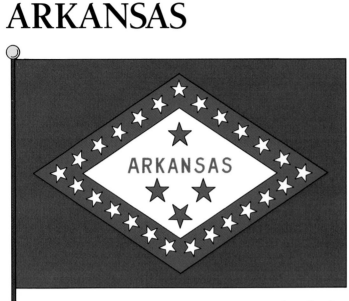

State flag official on
February 26, 1913

In 1912, a new U.S. battleship, called the *Arkansas*, was to be commissioned. This was a proud moment for the state. To commemorate the occasion, the Daughters of the American Revolution (DAR) voted unanimously to give a stand of **colors** (three flags) to the new ship. The flags to be given were a United States flag, a naval battle flag, and an Arkansas state flag. The Pine Bluff, Arkansas, chapter of the DAR wrote to the secretary of state asking for a copy of the official state flag. The secretary replied, "Arkansas has no state flag."

Thus began a movement to obtain a state flag. The DAR petitioned leading newspapers in the state to publish articles asking people to submit designs appropriate for a state flag. A committee would make the final choice. Each entry was supposed to include an explanation of the design but not the name of the artist. Out of 65 designs, the DAR unanimously selected that of a Pine Bluff woman, Miss Willie K. Hocker.

Hocker's design consists of a large white diamond bordered by a wide band of blue **charged** on a rectangular **field** of red. A commission later added the word *Arkansas* across the diamond and four blue stars. One star is above the state's name and three stars are below. Twenty-five white stars appear on the blue band.

The diamond design was chosen because Arkansas contains the only known diamond mine within the United States, and Arkansas's nickname is the "Diamond State."

Other aspects of the design also signify much of Arkansas's history. Red, white, and blue, the colors of the national flag, reflect Arkansas's patriotism. The blue star above the name *Arkansas* stands in memory of the state's membership in the Confederacy. The three blue stars below the state's name represent Spain, France, and the United States, the three nations to whom Arkansas has successively belonged. The three-star cluster also indicates that Arkansas was the third state carved from the territory that made up the Louisiana Purchase. The 25 white stars show that Arkansas was the 25th state to join the Union.

Arkansas came into the Union paired with another state, Michigan. This relationship is shown by the pair of stars on the lower angle of the blue band.

A joint resolution to adopt the design as the official state flag was passed by both houses of the general assembly in February 1913.

CALIFORNIA

*State flag official on
February 3, 1911*

California was under Mexican rule until 1846. When the United States declared war on Mexico because of a boundary dispute, Ezekiel "Stuttering" Merritt and a dozen settlers began a small revolution. Afraid that Mexico would force them to leave California, they captured a band of horses and rode north, fighting small pitched battles along the way. By the time they had crossed the Sacramento River and advanced to the upper Napa Valley, Merritt's forces had grown from 12 to about 35 persons. Early on the morning of June 14, 1846, Merritt took the poorly defended community of Sonoma by surprise and the Bear Flag Revolt officially began.

The revolutionary forces wanted a flag to replace the Mexican flag that had flown there and to let the world know about the revolt. They gathered odds and ends of cloth and materials to color the cloth. The white **field** of the flag, according to legend, was actually a woman's white petticoat. A red stripe—probably part of another lady's petticoat—was sewn across the field of white.

William Todd, a cousin of Mary Todd Lincoln, was an artist and pharmacist who had traveled west. Using red paint or berry juice and either a brush or a chewed stick, he drew a single red star in the **canton**, the upper corner next to the flagpole. On the white field near the bottom, he printed the words *California Republic* in black. Above the lettering, facing the star, he drew a crude likeness of a grizzly bear standing on all fours. Todd wanted to commemorate the magnificent creatures who greeted the pioneers, as well as to warn the Mexican army of the rebels' determination to gain independence.

California finally entered the Union as the 31st state on September 9, 1850. The original flag that Todd painted was preserved in San Francisco until 1906, when it was lost during an earthquake and fire.

On February 3, 1911, Governor Johnson signed a bill making the Bear Flag the state emblem, but as time passed, manufacturers of the Bear Flag began taking liberties when reproducing it. Finally, on June 14, 1953, Governor Earl Warren signed a bill to standardize the state flag. Today's flag resembles the original. The brown bear is pictured on a section of turf. Brown is the color of the grizzly bear, which became extinct in California in the early part of this century.

COLORADO

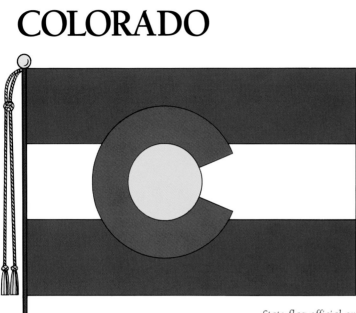

*State flag official on
June 5, 1911*

In 1876, when the United States was celebrating its 100th birthday, a new star was added to Old Glory. This star represented Colorado, nicknamed the "Centennial State." Years later, the Denver chapter of the Daughters of the American Revolution originated the state flag, and Andrew Carlisle Carson designed it. The design was approved by the general assembly on April 5, 1911, and it became official two months later, in June.

The state flag Carson designed—a red, white, blue, and gold banner—marks the history and resources of Colorado. The two bold, blue stripes depict the blue sky. The white stripe in the center stands for the snow-capped mountains. It also symbolizes Colorado's vast stores of silver, which have made it the richest silver-mining state in the Union.

The red *C* in Colorado's flag has several meanings, and it provides a reminder of the state's cultural and geographical roots. Within 50 years after Columbus discovered the New World, Spanish explorers, searching for gold, began pushing northward from Mexico. Instead of finding gold, however, they found the Cheyenne, the Arapahoe, and the Ute, the "red people" of the West. The Spaniards also found a turbulent river that sliced through rugged chasms and fertile valleys. Because of the color of the soil, the river was red. They named this river *Colorado,* meaning red or ruddy.

The ball of gold inside the red *C* represents both the year-round sunshine and the gold buried in the mountains.

The cords and tassels—one silver and one gold—which hang entwined from the flagstaff, represent the rich mines found in the state.

CONNECTICUT

*State flag official on
June 3, 1897*

The state flag of Connecticut officially dates from 1897. The design, however, was inspired by fervent patriots who lived a century before.

The Anne Warner Bailey chapter of the Daughters of the American Revolution (DAR) began the search for the present state flag of Connecticut. After DAR lobbying, a bill was introduced in the state assembly by Governor O. Vincent Coffin on May 29, 1895, and a special committee was appointed to prepare a flag. For two years the committee searched past records. They finally submitted the following design:

> A flag, the **field** of azure blue **charged** with a shield of **rococo** design of **argent** white silk, having embroidered in the center three grape vines, supported and bearing fruit in natural colors. The **bordure** to the shield shall be embroidered in two colors,

gold and silver. Below the shield shall be a white streamer, cleft at each end, bordered by gold and browns in fine lines and upon the streamer shall be embroidered in dark blue the motto *Qui Transtulit Sustinet*, "He who brought us over will sustain us."

The general assembly adopted the design for the state flag in 1897.

The motto on the flag is an adaptation of the 80th Psalm. The vines on the state seal symbolize the colonists, who crossed the ocean and transplanted their families in the wilderness in order to live in freedom and peace. The supports holding the vines stand for faith in God.

The word *Connecticut* is a Native American word meaning "long river." The state was settled and developed by the followers of Reverend Thomas Hooker.

DELAWARE

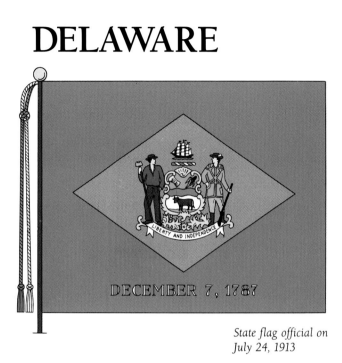

DECEMBER 7, 1787

State flag official on
July 24, 1913

Although Delaware had many unofficial flags, no attempt was made to adopt a state flag until 1913. During the colonial period, Delaware's troops were composed of British, Dutch, and Swedish settlers. They fought in both the French and Indian wars and the Revolutionary War. In the latter war, one Delaware regiment carried a banner of green silk with a **field** containing 13 alternating red and white horizontal stripes.

The flag displayed at the Delaware State Building, at the Centennial Exposition, was a white pennant with the word *Delaware* in bright blue letters. And in 1910, when the U.S.S. *Delaware* was commissioned and lay at anchor in the Delaware River, near Wilmington, still another flag was presented. That banner came closest to resembling the present state flag.

Finally, in 1913, state officials authorized a single design. Now the official state flag is a field of colonial blue, reminiscent of the blue hen, the official bird of the state.

A buff-colored diamond is in the center of the flag. Within the diamond is Delaware's coat of **arms**, as it appears on the state seal. The seal, adopted in 1777, shows a husbandman (farmer), holding a hoe in his right hand, and an American soldier, armed but at ease, supporting the shield. The shield bears a sheaf of wheat and an ear of corn. Across the middle of the shield is a strip of blue, representing the state's rivers. Below the blue strip is an ox standing in a meadow. A sailing ship above the shield represents the exports and imports that have passed through Delaware's ports, past and present.

The words *Liberty and Independence* are boldly printed on a ribbon draped beneath the shield and anchored firmly under the right heel of the farmer and the left heel of the soldier. The stance of the farmer and soldier indicate that both are necessary to keep liberty and independence intact.

In white, across the bottom, is the date *December 7, 1787*. It proudly proclaims that Delaware was the first of the original 13 states to ratify the Constitution.

FLORIDA

*State flag official on
May 21, 1985*

Florida entered the Union on March 3, 1845, as the 27th state. The original state flag of Florida was raised for the first and, as far as is known, the last time on June 25, 1845. A band played "Yankee Doodle" as this flag was hoisted for the inauguration of the first governor of Florida, William D. Moseley.

A group of Tallahassee citizens prepared this first flag, which included stars and stripes as part of the design. It was composed of five horizontal stripes of blue, orange, red, white, and green. In the center of the second stripe was a scroll with the words *Let Us Alone*.

The motto raised a furor. The Whigs, a political party preceding the Republicans, charged the Democrats with using a party motto on the state flag. The Democrats argued that it was not a party motto but an answer to France, who seemed reluctant to stay out of Florida's affairs.

New flag designs were immediately offered, but no agreement was reached. The design problem was then referred to a select committee which failed to submit a report on the matter. The designs gathered dust until November 30, 1860, when Governor Madison S. Perry signed an act calling for a secession convention. That same day, a bill was introduced to provide a national flag because Florida was getting ready to secede from the Union and could no longer use the Union flag.

On January 11, 1861, the day the official Ordinance of Secession was signed, a pale blue flag charged with three large stars appeared. The stars represented Florida, Mississippi, and South Carolina, states that had seceded. The flag had seven alternating red and white stripes, and along the center of the lower arc of a circle were 12 smaller, pale blue stars.

In February 1861, a bill was unanimously passed for an official state flag and six months later a design was adopted. This flag used three horizontal stripes of equal size. The flag's colors were blue, red, and white. Incorporated in the design was the motto *In God Is Our Trust* and, in smaller letters, the word *Florida*. Along the side of the banner there was an oak tree standing before the Gulf of Mexico, which was filled with sailing vessels. It is not recorded if this flag was ever raised over the capitol.

After the Civil War, new provisions were made for a state flag. In 1868, Florida's state seal was designed and impressed upon a white **field.** The seal shows the sun's rays, a palm tree, a steamboat on water, and a Native American woman scattering flowers in the foreground. Encircling the seal are the words *Great Seal of the State of Florida. In God We Trust.*

The state constitution of 1885 retained this state flag, and it was officially adopted in 1899. The design was revised in 1900 to add diagonal red bars reminiscent of the Confederate flag. That design has remained unchanged except for a 1966 amendment that allows greater flexibility in the dimensions of the flag and a few slight changes to the seal of the flag made in 1985.

GEORGIA

*State flag official on
July 1, 1956*

Officially, the state of Georgia has had five flags, but many other flags have been hoisted over Georgian soil.

The first flag accompanied Spanish explorers claiming the land for Spain. The flags of England and France followed, as those countries also attempted to claim the territory. Even the black flag of piracy may have been flown along the Georgia coast in the early 1700s.

During the Civil War, many flags represented the Confederate States, and each in turn was flown over Georgia. After the war was over, the United States' Stars and Stripes was raised again on Georgian soil.

Finally, in 1879, Georgia selected a flag of its own. On the **dexter** side, the side next to the flagpole, it had a vertical band of blue, emblematic of loyalty. The band occupied one-third of the entire flag. The remainder of the space was divided into three horizontal bands: the upper and lower bands were scarlet in color, and the middle band was white.

Although Georgia's citizens accepted the new design, they didn't totally approve of it. There were those who thought the state's flag should provide a memorial to the Confederacy while providing Georgia with a distinctive and historically significant flag.

Years later, this change was made. On July 1, 1956, Georgia raised a new state flag, designed by John Sammons Bell, chairman of the Democratic party. Bell's flag prominently displayed the battle flag of the Confederacy. On the vertical blue stripe is Georgia's seal. The closeness of the two symbols portrays the love and admiration that many Georgians have for their Confederate ancestors.

On the state seal, the three pillars of Wisdom, Justice, and Moderation support an arch bearing the word *Constitution.* Beneath the pillars is the original date of Georgia's entry into the Union, 1776.

HAWAII

*State flag official on
July 3, 1894
(Under the republic)*

In 1776 Captain James Cook, an English navigator, began a voyage that led to the discovery of the Hawaiian Islands by the Western world. Prior to Captain Cook's visit, Hawaiians did not display flags. They used such marks of distinction as the *kahili* (feathered cylinders on staffs) and the *puela* (a triangular shape decorating canoes). During the New Year festival (the *Makahiki*) they used symbols similar in form to Roman eagles.

In 1794, on his voyage around the world, Captain George Vancouver gave a British flag to King Kamehameha. The king raised the British flag on occasion, but he eventually realized that only by having his own flag would Hawaii be identified as his kingdom. Although it is not known exactly when a Hawaiian flag first appeared, a Russian named Kotzebue, who visited Hawaii aboard the ship *Rurik* in 1816, made reference to it.

By 1820, United States and British traders had arrived in great numbers and many Americans had become permanent settlers. There is no written history of Hawaii before British and U.S. settlers, so there is no written record of the flag's origin.

In 1843, Lord George Paulet, captain of the HBMS *Carysfort*, demanded surrender of King Kamehameha's government and destroyed all existing flags. However, Admiral Richard Thomas, Lord Paulet's superior officer, later restored the government, and the present Hawaiian flag was raised. Prior to 1845, Hawaii had had several flags of variant designs.

The earliest written history of the Hawaiian flag is contained in a letter to the editor of the Hawaiian newspaper *Kuokoa*. The letter appeared on January 1, 1862, and was translated by J. C. Lane.

> The Hawaiian flag was designed for King Kamehameha I, in the year 1816. As the King desired to send a vessel to China… Isaac Davis (the younger, known as Aikake) and Captain Alexander Adams…made this flag for the ship, which was a war vessel called the *Kaahumanu* carrying 16 guns, and was owned by King Kamehameha I. The flag having been made, the vessel sailed for Macao, China, where the flag was not credited nor recognized as a government flag….

The current flag consists of eight horizontal stripes, alternating white, red, and blue, beginning at the top. The eight stripes represent the major islands of the Hawaiian group. In the **canton** is the Union Jack, Great Britain's flag. It consists of a blue **field charged** with a compound cross of white and red. The British Union Jack is included out of consideration for Captain Vancouver, who gave the Islands their first flag.

Queen Liliuokalani was deposed by citizens of the United States who were living in Hawaii in 1893. They proclaimed Hawaii a republic, and in 1898, by request, the Islands were annexed by the United States as a territory.

In 1940, Hawaii requested full statehood, but the bombing of Pearl Harbor by the Japanese in 1941 and United States involvement in World War II delayed action. It wasn't until August 21, 1959, that Hawaii entered the Union as the 50th state. The new Hawaiian constitution accepted the territorial flag as the official state flag.

IDAHO

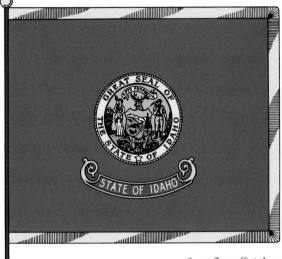

State flag official on
March 1, 1957

Idaho is a Shoshone word that means "sun coming down the mountain." The state was admitted to the Union in 1890.

While Idaho played only a minor part in the women's suffrage movement, the issue of women's rights played a decisive role in the design of the Idaho state seal, which was later to be an integral part of the state flag. The state seal, adopted on March 14, 1891, was based on a design submitted by Miss Emma Edwards, later Mrs. Emma Green. She described the seal in great detail:

> ....and as leading men and politicians agreed that Idaho would eventually give women the right to vote, and as mining was the chief industry, and the mining man the largest financial factor of the state at that time, I made the figure of the man the most prominent in the design, while that of the woman signifying justice, as noted by the scales, liberty, as denoted by the liberty

cap on the end of the spear, and equality with man, as denoted by her position at his side, also signifies freedom. The pick and the shovel held by the miner, the ledge of rock beside which he stands, as well as the pieces of ore scattered about his feet, all indicate the chief occupation of the state. The stamp mill in the distance…is also typical of mining interest of Idaho. The shield between the man and the woman is emblematic of the protection they unite in giving the state. The large fir or pine tree in the foreground, on the left side of the shield, and the sheaf of grain beneath the shield are emblematic of Idaho's agricultural resources while the cornucopias, or horns of plenty, refer to the horticultural resources. Idaho has a game law, which protects the elk and moose. The elk's head, therefore, rises above the shield. The state flower, the wild syringa or mock orange, grows at the woman's feet, while the ripened wheat grows as high as her shoulder. The star signifies a new light in the galaxy of states. The translation of the Latin motto [*Esto Perpetua*] is "It Is Perpetuated," or "It Is Forever." The river depicted in the shield is our mighty Snake or Shoshone River, a stream of great majesty.

The state flag was adopted in 1907. On it, the state seal was superimposed on a **field** of blue. A red scroll, on which was printed *State of Idaho*, was beneath the seal. Gold fringe bordered the flag.

After the legislature adopted the flag, the adjutant general of the state, Brigadier General C. A. Elmer, was supposed to issue specifications about the size of the flag and the color of the lettering. When he did this, he followed the general design adopted by the legislature, but he changed a few things. General Elmer's flag became the model that was used even though it did not follow the design prescribed by law. On March 15, 1927, the legislature changed the law to conform to the flag design that was actually in use. The present form of the Idaho state flag became official on March 1, 1957, after the legislature passed a law approving the design of the state seal.

ILLINOIS

*State flag official on
July 1, 1970*

At different times, France, Great Britain, and the United States had all owned the territory that later became Illinois. In 1800, it was still a part of the Northwest Territory, but the area within the present state boundaries was organized as a separate territory as early as 1809. Illinois entered the Union as the 21st state on December 3, 1818. Later it became known as the "Land of Lincoln."

Illinois has had two state flags. In 1912, Mrs. Ella Park Lawrence wanted to place an official state banner in Continental Memorial Hall in Washington, D.C., but Illinois had no official flag.

The following year, Mrs. Lawrence offered a prize of $25 to the Illinois chapters of the Daughters of the American Revolution. The prize was to be awarded for the best state flag design offered by any one of the chapters. Four judges were to select the winner. Of the 35 designs entered, Lucy

Derwent's, representing the Rockford chapter, was chosen. The flag she designed was made of white silk and had elements from the Illinois seal **charged** in the center.

The state seal was designed by Sharon Tyndale, the secretary of state in 1868. It replaced a previous seal.

On the seal designed by Tyndale, the shield is in a tilted position on the ground. The eagle is sitting on a boulder in a prairie, and a rising sun shines on a distant, eastern horizon. On the boulder are the dates *1868* and *1818*. A scroll of red ribbon flows from the eagle's bill, bearing the original motto *State Sovereignty—National Union.*

A flag bill did not reach the state legislature until 1915. The legislature was extremely busy that year, but the flag bill was pushed through quickly. The governor did not sign it, but the bill automatically became law on July 6, 1915. The first official flag of Illinois was made in Washington, D.C., and the design prevailed until the 1960s.

While serving in Vietnam, Chief Petty Officer Bruce McDaniel complained about his state flag's lack of distinction. He wrote to his state representative to request that the name of the state be added. His state representative, Jack Walker of Lansing, proposed a bill to amend the flag. The bill was passed by the general assembly and approved by Governor Richard B. Ogilvie on September 17, 1969.

The governor appointed a committee to develop specifications for the new flag. Mrs. Sanford Hutchison of Greenfield submitted a design that met all the committee's requirements. The present flag has the word *Illinois* in blue letters on a white **field,** and it carries an exact replica of Tyndale's state seal. This became the official flag of Illinois on July 1, 1970.

INDIANA

State flag official on
May 31, 1917

Congress created the Indiana Territory in 1800, and President John Adams appointed William Henry Harrison first territorial governor. The territory included the present states of Indiana, Illinois, Wisconsin, and parts of Michigan and Minnesota.

Early settlers in the area were frequently attacked by Native Americans. In 1811, Harrison defeated the Native Americans at the famous Battle of Tippecanoe. During the War of 1812, many Native Americans joined forces with the British, but Harrison again defeated them at the Battle of the Thames. After this battle, attacks stopped, and settlers were free to develop the territory. On December 11, 1816, Indiana entered the Union as the 19th state. Harrison, a battle hero, became president of the United States in 1841. He died only 30 days after taking office, however. Benjamin Harrison, William Henry Harrison's grandson and a resident of Indianapolis, became president in 1889.

Indiana grew as railroads came into the state and new industries developed. The Standard Oil Company and the United States Steel Corporation were two of the biggest. In 1911, the first Indianapolis 500 race was held. The event takes place every year and attracts large crowds. The state has undergone periods of economic growth as well as periods of decline. But Indiana has always responded well to its problems, and many areas are being redeveloped.

The state flag of Indiana was adopted by the general assembly in 1917. A design was chosen from several entries submitted to the Daughters of the American Revolution during the state's centennial celebration. The winning design was sumbitted by Paul Hadley of Mooresville, Indiana.

Hadley's design consisted of a gold torch **charged** in the center of a blue **field.** Gold stars surround the torch, which is a symbol of liberty and enlightenment. The outer circle of 13 gold stars represents the 13 original colonies. The five stars forming the inner circle represent the five states added to the Union after the Declaration of Independence. One larger star, immediately above the flame of the torch, stands for Indiana. The word *Indiana* appears directly above that star. The rays radiating from the torch symbolize the far-reaching effects of the light of freedom.

IOWA

State flag official on
March 29, 1921

Iowa was carved from the vast Louisiana Territory. It became a state in 1846, but Iowa did not officially adopt a state flag until 1921.

Steps were taken to prepare a flag in 1913, but years passed before any real progress was made. Then the women of Iowa took over the project. The Daughters of the American Revolution of Iowa submitted two designs to the governor for his approval. The first suggested a blue **field** upon which was **charged** the silver seal of Iowa. The second, submitted by Mrs. Dixie Gebhardt, was the design that was selected.

Gebhardt's design bears three vertical bars: blue, white, and red. The white center bar is slightly larger than the other two. The three colors reflect the flags of both the United States and France, since both countries played a role in the history of Iowa. The flag depicts Iowa's occupation by Native Americans, its discovery by the French, Jefferson's purchase of the land from Napoleon, and Iowa's admission into the Union.

The broad white stripe represents Iowa in its virgin beauty with unbroken wilderness, abundant flowers, and unspoiled nature. In the center of the white stripe, the word *Iowa* is printed in bold red letters. Brilliant red is used to commemorate both the Native Americans and the sacrifices made by Iowa's first settlers.

The soaring eagle on the flag was inspired by the Iowa state seal and by the national bird of the United States. In its beak is a blue streamer with the motto *Our Liberties We Prize and Our Rights We Will Maintain* in white letters.

The design was accepted with slight modifications, and the Daughters of the American Revolution presented a banner to each of the eight state regiments preparing for overseas duty in World War I. The first banner was sent to the Third Iowa Regiment in New York City in November 1917. They became part of the 168th U.S. Regiment, part of the Rainbow Division. The flag was not unpacked until the regiment reached France. There, in an old chateau that had been taken over for regimental headquarters, the new state flag was formally presented to Colonel E. R. Bennett on New Year's Day, 1918. Thereafter it was carried at the head of the regiment.

A bill to make the DAR design the official state flag came before the 38th general assembly in January, 1919, but it was not passed. One of the Iowa soldiers who was serving in France wrote home to his father. In his letter, he said that the United States flag was sufficient for all purposes, and a state flag was unnecessary. The boy's father read the letter aloud to the state senate, and both houses of the general assembly (the state senate and house of representatives) voted against the state-flag bill.

However, the Iowa DAR authorized an eastern flag-making firm to produce the flag anyway, and thousands of them were sold. The small commission derived from the sale was passed on to a relief fund.

Two years later, on March 29, 1921, the 39th general assembly officially adopted the Iowa flag.

KANSAS

*State flag official on
June 30, 1963*

In 1803 the United States acquired the land that is now Kansas as part of the Louisiana Purchase. Also included in the history of Kansas is the crucial role the state played in the struggle against slavery. In Congress during the 1850s, Northerners and Southerners disagreed about whether or not new states and territories should allow slavery. In 1854, Senator Stephen A. Douglas thought of a way for Congress to create new territories while avoiding the slavery question. Under the Kansas-Nebraska Bill, the idea of "squatter sovereignty" (also known as popular sovereignty) allowed settlers (sometimes called squatters) to decide the slavery question for themselves. This bill ended a Congressional debate that had kept territories from being admitted to the Union. Kansas became a territory on May 30, 1854.

Kansas chose to outlaw slavery but its sister state, Missouri, had been admitted to the Union in 1821 as a slave state. A border war broke out along the Kansas-Missouri border. This battle attracted the attention of the entire United States as proslavery and antislavery groups fought for political control. Finally, the antislavery group gained control of the state legislature. Kansas was admitted as a free state in 1861, thus becoming the 34th state to join the Union.

Within a few weeks, the Civil War broke out, and Kansas became involved in violence again. Confederate raiders attacked, but Kansans fought back. After the war ended in 1865, many Union veterans settled in Kansas.

The Kansas state flag, adopted by the legislature in March 1927, conveys much historic significance. The design includes both the inner field of the state seal and the military **crest**. The sunflower is the official flower of Kansas. The open frankness of its face is indicative of the fearlessness with which Kansas faces its problems and solves them. The bar beneath the sunflower signifies the Louisiana Purchase. Together, these symbols form the military crest of Kansas. The 34 stars stand for Kansas as the 34th state.

Within the state seal, the rising sun represents the east. The hills on the seal identify terrain near Fort Riley. Here the official flag was first displayed by Governor Ben S. Paulen in 1927. The steamboat represents commerce. The buffalo and the Native American, the oxen and the prairie schooners (covered wagons), depict the advance of the frontier. The log cabin, the plowed fields, and the plowman represent agriculture.

The blue **field** or background of the flag stands for the loyalty and steadfastness of the people of Kansas. The azure and yellow of the seal symbolize the contributions of many lands and commonwealths to produce a contented, harmonious citizenry.

The motto *Ad Astra per Aspera*, "To the Stars through Difficulties," describes the seven years of border warfare before Kansas joined the Union. The name *Kansas*, in big gold letters, was added in 1961. It proclaims pride in this great agricultural and industrial state. The law was amended again in 1963 to modify specifications of the flag.

KENTUCKY

*State flag official on
June 14, 1962*

The state of Kentucky is steeped in legends and traditions. The region was named from a combination of Native American words meaning "dark and bloody ground." The name is said to refer to fierce wars that took place among the Native American tribes who populated the area early in the history of the United States.

Several English and French explorers probably visited the Kentucky area in the late 1600s and early 1700s. By 1776, several hunters and scouts, including Daniel Boone, had come into the region, and settlements soon followed. Kentucky became a county of Virginia and many Virginians moved into the Kentucky region. Population increased and Kentucky became a territory in 1790. Kentucky joined the Union as the 15th state on June 1, 1792. The new state continued to grow with settlers from Virginia and the Carolinas. Kentucky's waterways also played an important role in the rapid growth of the state since farmers used steamboats to ship crops and livestock to market along the Ohio and Mississippi rivers.

At the outset of the Civil War, Kentucky remained neutral, not wishing to support either side. But Confederate troops invaded Kentucky in 1861. Several battles were fought and both sides suffered heavy losses. Finally, the victory of the Union troops at the Battle of Perryville, in 1862, secured the state for the Union. Kentucky did not secede.

The Kentucky flag, approved by the state legislature on March 26, 1918, is described as a flag made of navy blue silk or bunting. The seal of the Commonwealth of Kentucky, encircled by a wreath of goldenrod, is embroidered, printed, or stamped on the center of the blue **field.**

The state seal, adopted in 1792, depicts a statesman and a frontiersman embracing. The state's motto, *United We Stand, Divided We Fall,* appears above and below them. Originally, the name *Kentucky* ran across the top of the seal, but by state legislation on April 6, 1893, the wording was changed to read the *Commonwealth of Kentucky*.

A senate bill, passed by the general assembly on March 5, 1962, states that now the official flag may also be made of nylon, wool, or other suitable material. The emblem at the head of the flag staff is that of the Kentucky cardinal in an alert but restful pose.

Flying the Kentucky state flag at all state buildings and installations, including public school buildings, is considered proper and is encouraged.

LOUISIANA

State flag official on
July 1, 1912

Louisiana entered the Union in 1812, and exactly one hundred years later the state legislature officially adopted a state flag.

Flags of many different nations were raised over this territory before Louisiana became one of the United States. In 1682, the French explorer René-Robert Cavalier, Sieur de la Salle and a band of 50 men claimed the territory for France. They planted a French flag of heraldic design, and La Salle named the vast Mississippi Valley region *Louisiana*, in honor of the French king, Louis XIV.

France, however, became disappointed with the small income produced by the colony. In 1762, France secretly ceded Louisiana to Spain. This act was kept secret because officials were certain that the French colonists in Louisiana would become angry if they knew their land had been given to Spain.

However, the French colonists learned about the transfer in 1764, and their contempt for Spanish authority resulted in several uprisings. Colonists demanded that the Spanish flag be replaced with the French flag. Although a band of Frenchmen drove out the Spanish governor in 1768, Spain took firm control of the territory in 1769. Spain returned Louisiana to France in 1800.

In 1801, President Thomas Jefferson sent Robert R. Livingston, U.S. Ambassador to France, to negotiate the purchase of Louisiana. Negotiations were completed in 1803 when the United States bought the Louisiana Territory for $15 million. In December 1803, the flag of the United States was raised over the territory.

Other flags followed, including the West Florida Lone Star flag, the Independent Louisiana flag (Louisiana functioned for six weeks as an independent nation before joining the Confederacy), and the Confederate flag. At the end of the Civil War, the Union's Stars and Stripes was again hoisted over the state.

Before the current state flag was authorized, there were several variations of the pelican flag. The **field** was sometimes red, sometimes blue. It was suggested at a convention in 1861 that the blue and white pelican flag be adopted, but it was not until after Reconstruction (the period following the Civil War) that the new design was used. Not until July 1, 1912, did legislative action make the state flag official.

The blue field signifies truth. The motto, *Union, Justice & Confidence,* is self-explanatory. The design of the pelican feeding her young shows the state's role as protector of its people and resources. There is a legend that in time of famine, the mother pelican plucks the flesh from her own breast to nourish her starving fledglings. Thus, from the bosom of Louisiana, from the heart of her fertile fields, her children are sustained by bounteous harvests.

MAINE

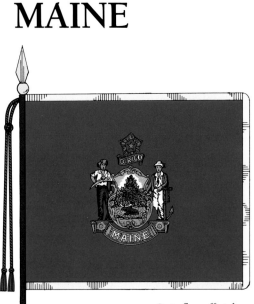

*State flag official on
February 24, 1909*

The flag of Maine was adopted by the state legislature in 1909. It bears the state **arms charged** on a blue **field.** The blue is the same shade as that used in the national flag.

The arms consist of a shield, supporters, ribbons, and a star. The lower portion of the shield shows water, representative of Maine's deeply indented, rockbound coastline, its fine natural harbors, and its numerous rivers.

The upper section of the shield shows the sky. A huge pine tree, representing Maine's forests, stands in the foreground. Maine is nicknamed the "Pine Tree State," since forests cover 90 percent of its land. Below the pine tree is a moose that symbolizes Maine's undisturbed wildlife areas.

A farmer and a seaman support the shield. On the heraldic right of the shield (to the viewer's left), a farmer with a scythe symbolizes the agriculture of Maine. On the other side, a seaman, leaning on an anchor, represents fishing and commerce. The sea and the people who sail it have always played a vital part in the history of Maine.

Below the shield is a ribbon bearing the word *Maine*. Above the shield, the North Star represents Maine's northern location. The star rests on a smaller ribbon bearing the motto *Dirigo,* "I Direct."

The origin of the state's name is somewhat unclear. Some believe it means *mainland* because early English explorers used the term *the main* to distinguish the mainland from the offshore islands. However, others believe the name was originally derived from a province in France.

Maine received colonists 13 years before the Pilgrims landed at Plymouth Rock, but the severe weather and their lack of supplies forced them to return to England. The first permanent settlements were established in the 1620s, but Maine, the 23rd state, did not attain statehood until March 15, 1820. Today Maine is an important farming and fishing state. It has the largest lobster catch of any state, and the beautiful, rocky coast of Maine attracts many visitors every year. Forests are also important in Maine and cover almost 90 percent of the state. Wood-processing forms an important part of the state's economy.

MARYLAND

*State flag official on
March 9, 1904*

In 1608, Maryland was explored by Captain John Smith. In 1632, King Charles I of England granted the land to George Calvert, the first Lord Baltimore. When Calvert died shortly thereafter, the land went to his son Cecil, the second Lord Baltimore. Cecil then appointed his brother Leonard as governor of the colony. The colony was named in honor of Queen Henrietta Maria, the wife of King Charles. The first settlement was made at St. Mary's, on the Potomac River. The laws of the colony were based on the idea of religious tolerance.

The design of the Maryland state flag is based on the coats of **arms** of two families. The black and gold quarters of the flag are the arms of Lord Baltimore's father's family, the Calverts. The red and white quarters are those of the family of Lord Baltimore's mother, the Crosslands. Since she was her father's heiress, Lord Baltimore's mother had the right to quarter her arms with those of her husband. The cross that appears in the flag is known in heraldry as botonée—a cross having a cluster of balls or knobs at the end of each arm.

The design for the state flag was taken from the insignia in Lord Baltimore's seal, which dates from the 1630s. The insignia was first included in a flag about 1638. The state flag was officially adopted in 1904.

Black and gold are the official state colors of Maryland, and even nature seems to agree with Maryland's color choices. The black-eyed Susan, the official flower, grows profusely in the state. The brilliant flower starts blooming in early July and reproduces Maryland's colors, black and gold. The blossom usually has 13 petals, which can symbolize the 13 original states, one of which was Maryland.

The Baltimore oriole was officially named the state bird in 1947. Its feathers are a vivid black and orange.

Maryland has the oldest state capitol building in the United States that is still in use daily. Work on the building began just as the Revolution was brewing, in 1772. The building was completed during the Revolutionary War, and the Revolution was officially ended within its walls.

MASSACHUSETTS

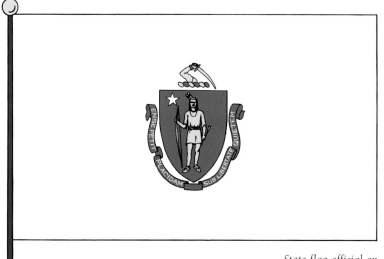

*State flag official on
November 1, 1971*

A Massachusetts state flag was first created in 1908. The flag, which has a white **field**, originally had a different design on each side.

In 1908, the reverse side had a green pine tree upon a blue shield. The pine-tree insignia represented the numerous flags that have been flown throughout the stormy history of Massachusetts. The design of one such flag was passed and approved by the revolutionary council as early as April 1776. The council stated that the color should be white with a green pine tree superimposed. The inscription was to read *Appeal to Heaven*.

On the other side of the 1908 flag was a shield bearing the figure of a Native American man. (This now appears on both sides of the flag.) He is holding a bow in his right hand, and an arrow pointing downward in his left hand. In the upper corner of the shield, above his right arm, is a white star with five points.

A **crest** above the shield consists of an arm bent at the elbow, hand grasping a broadsword. The crest is symbolic of the state motto.

The motto, inscribed on a scroll around the shield, reads *Ense Petit Placidam sub Libertate Quietem*. It is the second of two lines written by Algernon Sidney, a 17th-century English soldier and politician. The motto, adopted in 1775 by the provincial congress, means "By the Sword We Seek Peace, but Peace Only under Liberty."

The Norsemen were probably the first white explorers to touch the shores of Massachusetts. Fishermen from Spain and France and navigators from England followed. But the first important European colony was originated by the Pilgrims, who were seeking religious freedom.

The first blood for the cause of American independence was shed in Massachusetts. The embattled farmers—the minutemen—warned by the historic rides of Paul Revere and William Dawes, engaged the British in battles at Lexington and Concord. There, a minuteman fired "the shot heard 'round the world."

Massachusetts, one of the original 13 colonies, was the sixth state to ratify the Constitution.

MICHIGAN

State flag official on
August 1, 1911

It is symbolic and fitting that the first flag of Michigan was "born" on George Washington's birthday, February 22, in the same year that Michigan entered the Union, 1837.

On that day, Michigan's first governor, 23-year-old Stevens T. Mason (nicknamed the "Boy Governor"), presented a flag representing the state to a militia known as the Brady Guards of Detroit. The flag consisted of a **field** of blue with a portrait of the governor **charged** on one side, while the other side bore the state seal framed by a Brady Guard on one side and a woman on the other.

General Lewis Cass, who was territorial governor from 1813 to 1831, designed the state seal. Cass sought to capture the beauty of Michigan in his design. Also, he had fought in the War of 1812, and he was impressed with the strategic location of Michigan. In 1835, he presented his drawings for the seal of the forthcoming state to the secretary of the territory. The design was adopted on June 2, 1835. Similar flags were used by Michigan troops until 1865.

When the state's soldiers returned from southern battlefields after the Civil War, Michigan officially adopted a new state military flag. The front or **obverse** side bore the state coat of **arms**. The reverse side was charged with the coat of arms of the United States. This flag was first unfurled on the Fourth of July at the ceremony honoring war dead. The design prevailed until April 11, 1911, when the state legislature passed a law fixing the current design, which retains the state arms but omits the national arms.

The blue **field** of the flag is charged with Cass's design. The shield bears the motto *Tuebor,* "I Will Defend." Below the motto is a scene composed of a grassy plain, a turbulent lake, and a rising sun. There is a man whose right arm is raised, and whose left arm holds a firearm. This signifies the state's readiness to defend its rights.

An American eagle rises above the shield. The eagle's right talon holds an olive branch with 13 fruit; its left talon holds a sheaf of 3 arrows. Above the eagle's head is a ribbon with the United States motto, *E Pluribus Unum,* "Out of Many, One."

The shield is supported by an elk and a moose, both rampant or rearing. Beneath their hooves is a scroll bearing the words *Si Quaeris Peninsulam Amoenam Circumspice,* "If You Seek a Pleasant Peninsula, Look Around You." The officials did look about them, and they decided that General Cass had described the natural beauties of Michigan quite well.

The word *Michigan* comes from *michigama,* the Chippewa word meaning "great or large lake."

MINNESOTA

*State flag official on
March 19, 1957*

In 1893, the Minnesota legislature passed a law adopting a state flag. The design for the flag was presented by a commission of women appointed for that purpose. They chose a design by Mrs. Edward H. Center of Minneapolis.

The flag had two different sides, white on the **obverse** (front) and light blue on the reverse side. The state seal was **charged** in the center of the obverse side only, and the flag was bound by yellow fringe on three sides.

The state seal pictures a pioneer farmer plowing, his gun and powder horn within reach on a nearby stump. He is looking back at a Native American who is riding a galloping horse toward the setting sun. At the top of the picture is the French motto, *L'Etoile du Nord,* "The Star of the North."

The seal was bordered by a flower wreath of lady's slippers on a light blue background. The three dates that were woven into the wreath were *1858* (the date Minnesota became a state), *1819* (the date Fort Snelling—the state's original fur-trading station—was established), and *1893* (the year the first state flag was adopted).

The flower wreath was tied at the bottom with a bow of red ribbon, the end of which extended across the flag. The state's name was printed in gold letters.

Around the wreath were 19 gold stars, arranged to suggest the five points of a star. The larger star at the top symbolized Minnesota, the "North Star State." There were 19 stars because Minnesota was the 19th state to enter the Union after the original colonies. (It was the 32nd state to enter the Union.)

That flag was expensive to produce and therefore wasn't displayed very often. Many people suggested changing the design. Accordingly, in 1955, a committee consisting of five senators and five representatives was appointed to study the issue. In 1957, they approached the legislature with a modified design.

The revised and current flag has a smaller seal placed on a background of royal blue. The bow has been removed and the word *Minnesota*, printed in red, appears in the border of the seal. The 19 gold stars are placed closer to the seal and a gold line encircles the entire design.

This flag design was approved by the legislature on March 18, 1957, and it became official the following day.

MISSISSIPPI

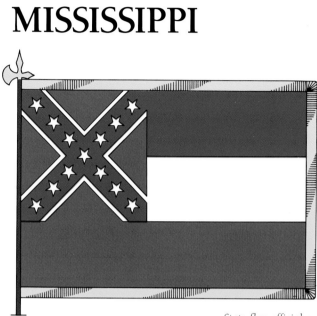

*State flag official on
February 7, 1894*

The flag of Mississippi was designed by a committee headed by General W. T. Martin. It was adopted by the state legislature in February, 1894, following the Reconstruction period after the Civil War.

During the Civil War, Mississippi seceded from the Union and joined the Confederate States. After the war, Mississippi surrendered and rejoined the Union. Although some Mississippians still felt loyalty to the Confederate cause, the state leaders petitioned the United States Congress for pardon for their act of secession.

Because of Mississippi's divided sense of loyalty, its state flag became both a memorial to the men who gave their lives in the Civil War and a celebration of being a part of the United States once again.

The flag makes use of the national colors—red, white, and blue. A union square, two-thirds the **hoist** (width) of the flag, serves as background for a broad blue **saltire.** The saltire is bordered with white and emblazoned with 13 five-pointed stars, which correspond to the 13 original colonies. This corner of the flag is an exact reproduction of the Confederate battle flag. The remaining **field** of the flag is divided into three bars of equal width, the upper one blue, the middle one white, and the lower one red. The flag is fringed with gold.

Mississippi was discovered and mapped by the Spanish explorer Hernando de Soto in 1541. De Soto died on the Mississippi River and was buried beneath its waters. The state takes its name from the river. *Mississippi* means "great water" or "father of waters" in the language of the Native Americans who lived in the region. Although historians do not agree which tribe originated the name, most agree it was made up of two words, *mescha* meaning "great" and *cebe* meaning "river."

Mississippi, the 20th state to enter the Union, joined on December 10, 1817. In 1861, it was the second state to secede, and it was among the last to be restored to the Union.

MISSOURI

*State flag official on
March 22, 1913*

The state flag of Missouri was conceived, designed, and created by Mrs. Marie Elizabeth Watkins Oliver of Cape Girardeau. The wife of former Senator R. B. Oliver, Marie Oliver saw her design officially adopted by the 47th general assembly in 1913.

The Missouri state flag has three horizontal stripes, red at the top, white in the center, and blue at the bottom. The state coat of **arms** is **charged** in the center of the flag. The state seal and coat of arms were designed by a committee of legislators, including Chauncy Smith, James Alcorn, Elias Elston, and, according to some sources, Robert William Wells. The seal was adopted by the legislature and signed into law in 1822.

Half of the shield is occupied by the coat of arms of the United States. The U.S. coat of arms consists of an eagle with arrows in its left talon and an olive branch in its right talon. Above it is a constellation of stars representing the original 13 states. The other half of the Missouri coat of arms shows a grizzly bear and a new moon. The great grizzly, once native to Missouri, is noted for its strength and size. The red background, against which the bear stands, represents courage. Together, the two sections indicate the connection between the state and federal governments—each depending upon the other. Surrounding the shield is a band with the words *United We Stand Divided We Fall.*

Over the coat of arms is a **crest** and a helmet, which represent strength. On the crest, 24 stars symbolize Missouri's admission into the Union on August 10, 1821, as the 24th state. The stars are pictured on a patch of blue sky.

The coat of arms is supported by Missouri grizzlies rearing on hind legs and securing a scroll inscribed with the Latin motto *Salus Populi Suprema Lex Esto,* "Let the Welfare of the People Be the Supreme Law." Under the scroll are the Roman numerals MDCCCXX (1820). The date probably refers to the passage of the Missouri Compromise, an act of Congress that permitted Missouri to enter the Union as a slave state.

Originally explored by René-Robert Cavelier, Sieur de la Salle, in the name of France, Missouri was included in the huge tract of land which the United States bought from France in 1803—the Louisiana Purchase. The territory rapidly became known as the "Gateway to the West" because of its extensive river traffic. The Missouri and the Mississippi rivers merge within Missouri's boundaries.

MONTANA

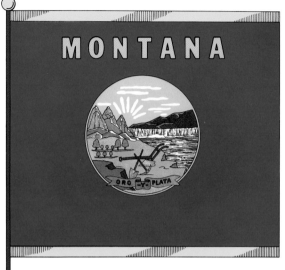

*State flag official on
July 1, 1981*

Though not officially the state flag of Montana, a blue banner **charged** with the seal of the state and bearing the words *First Montana Infantry U.S.V.* was carried by the Montana Volunteers in the Spanish-American War of 1898.

This original, handmade banner has been preserved by the Historical Society of Montana. Although the dark blue silk of the **field** is now tattered and faded, the great seal, which was so painstakingly embroidered, is still in perfect condition.

When the ninth legislative assembly gathered in Helena in 1905, Representative Jacob M. Kennedy of Silver Bow County introduced a bill to adopt this banner as the state flag. The only change the bill called for was the removal of the military inscription. Kennedy's bill passed unanimously. In 1981, the name of the state was added to create the current flag design.

The basic design for the seal was submitted by Francis McGee Thompson, a representative from Beaverhead County. The first legislative assembly at Bannack, then the territorial capital, approved Thompson's design during the winter of 1864-65. His design for the seal was based on life around him.

The Montana state seal contains a plow, a miner's pick, and a shovel. These symbols honor agriculture and mineral wealth. A mountain scene and the Great Falls of the Missouri River appear in the background. The pine trees pictured in the foreground represent the evergreens that abound on the mountain slopes.

The mountain scenery is symbolic of the state, which, because it is crossed diagonally by the Rocky Mountain range, was named for its mountainous surface. At the foot of the scene is a scroll with the Spanish words *Oro y Plata*, "Gold and Silver."

Montana was admitted to the Union as the 41st state in 1889. It has been nicknamed the "Big Sky Country."

NEBRASKA

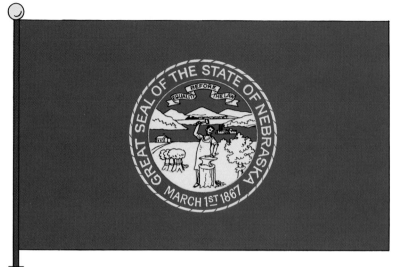

*State flag official on
April 2, 1925*

Not until 1925 did Nebraska's legislature designate an official banner to be used as the state flag. The passage of the state flag bill was a result of an intensive movement led by Mrs. Benjamin G. Miller of Crete, Nebraska. She and a number of other patriotic citizens urged Governor Adam McMullen to approve the bill.

Representative J. Lloyd McMaster of Lancaster County introduced the bill, which stipulates that the flag should consist of the great seal of the state **charged** in gold and silver on a **field** of national blue.

The state seal was first adopted in 1867. It depicts a blacksmith in the foreground, representing both the mechanical arts and the hardy pioneers. Shocks of corn and grain represent the agriculture of the state. The cabin symbolizes the settlers who came to the land. A steamboat represents river transportation, which was of major importance at the time the state was first settled.

A train heading toward the Rocky Mountains is a tribute to the Union Pacific Railroad. Nebraska was still a territory when the track was being laid for the "iron horse." The people who poured into this territory, either to help build the rail line or to service those who were building it, greatly swelled the population. Many stayed to help build the state of Nebraska.

The Rocky Mountains appear in the background of the seal. Nebraska is a state of rolling prairies sloping upward from the Missouri River to the foothills of the Rockies.

The motto *Equality before the Law* appears on a ribbon near the top of the seal. The words *Great Seal of the State of Nebraska, March 1st, 1867* appear around the seal to commemorate the date Nebraska entered the Union.

NEVADA

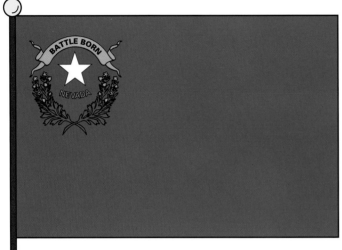

State flag official on
October 1, 1991

Nevada's first flag was designed by Governor John Sparks and Colonel Harry Day in 1905, about the same time the second transcontinental railroad line was wending its way through southern Nevada.

The **field** of the first flag was cobalt blue and the name *Nevada* was inscribed in the center. Above the state's name was the word *Silver* and below was the word *Gold,* printed appropriately in silver and gold. Undoubtedly, this design was greatly influenced by the Comstock lode, a rich deposit of gold and silver ore discovered in Nevada in 1859.

Seventeen five-pointed stars appeared between the words *Silver* and *Nevada* and 17 more between the words *Nevada* and *Gold.* There was also one larger star on each side of the state's name. The 36 stars represented Nevada becoming the 36th state.

This flag was replaced, however, by a second flag. The new banner depicted many industries, as well as the different geographical areas of the state. Colorful though it was, the second flag proved much too expensive to reproduce.

In 1929 state legislators passed an act to establish the third flag. This flag, with the exception of a 1991 change in the placement of the word *Nevada* on the flag, is the one that is used today. The body of the current flag is cobalt blue. It is **charged** with two sprays of sagebrush. The sagebrush stems are crossed to form a half-wreath. Sagebrush served both cattle and humans in Nevada: it provided food for the cow and medicine for the rancher. Early pioneers learned from Native Americans how to use the plant as a tonic. Sagebrush is also symbolic of the vast desert valleys within the state.

In the center of the spray is a five-pointed, silver star. The word *Nevada* formerly appeared between the points of the star. This, however, was changed in 1991, and the word *Nevada* is now underneath the star. This was done to make the state's name easier to read. Above the star is a golden yellow scroll bearing the word *Battle Born* in black letters. The words signify Nevada's admission to the Union during the Civil War. The silver star and golden scroll are symbolic of the wealth hidden beneath Nevada's numerous mountain ranges.

The word *Nevada* means "snow covered" in Spanish. The state was originally explored by the Spaniards. In 1848 the United States acquired the Nevada region from Mexico. Nevada became part of the Utah Territory and remained so until 1861, when Congress created the territory of Nevada. President Lincoln declared Nevada the 36th state on October 31, 1864.

NEW HAMPSHIRE

*State flag official on
January 1, 1932*

New Hampshire's earliest flags were those carried by the Second New Hampshire Regiment of the Continental Army during the Revolutionary War. Nicknamed "Rogers' Rangers," this group fought in the French and Indian wars, and they were among the first to take part in the Revolution. The words of General John Stark, who led the regiment, provided New Hampshire with its motto: *Live Free or Die*

The first official state flag of New Hampshire was adopted on February 24, 1909, although the general design it bore had been in use since 1784.

The present flag was modified by an act of the state legislature on May 1, 1931, when changes were made in the state seal. The act, which became effective on January 1, 1932, dictates that the flag "shall be of a blue **field** and shall bear upon its center, in suitable proportion and colors, a representation of the state seal. This seal is to be surrounded by a wreath of laurel leaves with nine stars interspersed."

The seal pictures the frigate *Raleigh*, one of the first ships built for the United States Navy during the Revolutionary War. A wreath of laurel, an ancient symbol of fame, honor, and victory, surrounds the *Raleigh*.

On the outer rim of the seal, nine stars show that New Hampshire was the ninth state to ratify the Constitution. John Langdon and Nicholas Gilman signed the Constitution for the state of New Hampshire on June 21, 1788. The stars before and after the year *1776* only separate the date from the words *Seal of the State of New Hampshire*.

NEW JERSEY

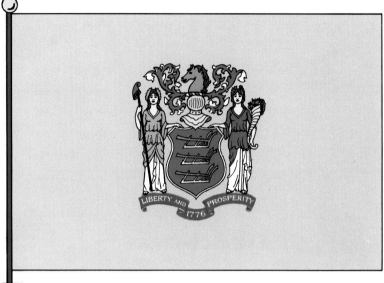

*State flag official on
March 26, 1896*

Indirectly, New Jersey's state flag was based on an order by General George Washington. It was the custom in Britain for each army regiment to have two regimental flags (known as **colors**), and the Continental Army followed this tradition. On October 2, 1779, Washington established the background color to be used for the second flag of each regiment. For New Jersey and New York, this was to be buff, a color similar to that used for the facings of the troops' uniforms. (Buff may have been chosen in error to correspond to the orange of the Dutch flag, which once flew over parts of New Jersey.) In 1896, the state decided to use buff for the background of its state flag, the only flag of this shade among the flags of the 50 states.

The center of the New Jersey flag bears the state coat of arms, which was designed in 1776 by Eugene du Simitiere. Du Simitiere also worked on the seal of the United States.

New Jersey's shield is supported by two female figures, Ceres and Liberty. Ceres, the goddess of agriculture, holds a cornucopia in her left hand. Traditionally, she represents prosperity and abundance. Liberty or Freedom carries a pole bearing a liberty cap (a close-fitting, cone-shaped cap used as a symbol of liberty) in her right hand.

The helmet on top of the shield was disputed by early legislators. Many of them contended that it symbolized the tyranny the colonies had just fought against. The designer argued that it was a symbol of the sovereignty the state had achieved as a result of the revolution.

Above the helmet is a horse's head, which is emblematic of speed, strength, and usefulness in war and commerce.

The motto *Liberty and Prosperity* was not in the original design, but became part of the seal through common usage. New Jersey's motto was officially incorporated and adopted in 1928.

NEW MEXICO

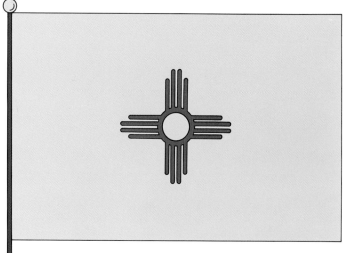

State flag official on
March 15, 1925

On January 6, 1912, a mass meeting was held in the plaza at Santa Fe. The crowd cheered about a victory for which New Mexico had been fighting for more than 60 years. President Taft had just signed the bill granting statehood to New Mexico.

On March 19, 1915, a state flag with a turquoise blue **field** was approved. Turquoise was first mined by the Native Americans, and it had always been sacred to them because it represented "sky powers."

A miniature flag of the United States was in the upper left-hand corner of the flag. It designated the national loyalty of the people of New Mexico. In the upper right-hand corner was the figure 47, the order of New Mexico's admission to the Union.

In the lower right-hand corner was the seal of New Mexico. The state seal is essentially the same as the one designed for the territory of New

Mexico in 1851 and adopted in 1887. It consists of the American eagle sheltering the Mexican eagle, which holds a serpent in its beak and cactus in its talons. The cactus and the serpent are based on an ancient Aztec legend. The American eagle grasps arrows in its talons. The words *New Mexico*, in white, were **charged** at a slant across the center of the 1915 flag.

This flag was very elaborate, expensive, and difficult to reproduce. A contest for a new design was held under the supervision of the Daughters of the American Revolution, and a new design submitted by Dr. Harry E. Mera of the New Mexico Archaeological Society was chosen. The design was adopted on March 15, 1925.

The present flag represents a blend of cultures. Its field of bright yellow is charged with the ancient Zia sun symbol. The Zias were a part of the Pueblo tribe located on the north bank of the James River. The brilliant yellow and red are reminiscent of the Spanish flag that flew over the land when the first explorers came into this region.

NEW YORK

State flag official on
April 2, 1901

Until the year 1881, there was much confusion about the correct flag for the state of New York. The purported flag was white with a beaver in the center. From 1858 onward, the flag had many variations, but primarily it was a "State flag made of white bunting, twelve feet **fly** by ten feet **hoist**, bearing in the centre the **arms** of the state of New York."

The color white, however, did not always remain a true white. Some people pointed out that Washington himself had selected buff as the color for the second regimental flag of New York and had issued a general order to that effect. (The New York and New Jersey Continental regiments had buff facings on blue uniforms during the Revolution.) Major Asa B. Gardiner worked to get approval for a buff-colored flag, and on April 8, 1896, he was successful.

However, a **field** of buff was unusual in a flag, and opposition to the color soon arose. By 1901, the fight to change the color of the flag's field from buff to blue was in full swing. State Historian Hugh Hastings led the battle. On March 27, 1901, Hastings wrote a letter of protest to Governor B. B. Odell. The historian argued that buff faded easily and that it was the recognized color of quarantine throughout the world.

Hastings went on to argue that both the Spanish and Chinese flags used yellow. A few weeks before Hasting's letter of protest, Chinese Minister Wi Ting Fang had reviewed the 23rd regiment in Brooklyn, and he had mistaken the state flag of New York for a Chinese flag flown to honor him.

Hastings won the argument. On April 2, in chapter 229 of the Laws of 1901, the color of the New York state flag was changed to blue.

The state coat of arms was made official in chapter 12 of the Laws of 1778. The shield is a landscape in which the sun is rising in splendor from behind a range of three mountains. The middle mountain is the highest of the three. In the lower portion of the shield is a ship and a sloop under sail. They are about to pass each other on a river bordered below by a grassy shore. The scene is produced in natural colors.

Above the shield is a world globe that reveals the North Atlantic Ocean. An American eagle is perched on top of the globe. Two female figures are supporting the shield. They are standing on a ribbon with the Latin word *Excelsior,* "Highest," written on it.

On one side is the figure of Liberty. In her right hand is a staff and on the staff is balanced a liberty cap, a close-fitting, cone-shaped cap used as a symbol of liberty.

On the other side is the figure of Justice. Her eyes are blindfolded, and in her right hand is a straight sword, held erect. In her left hand, she holds the scales of justice.

NORTH CAROLINA

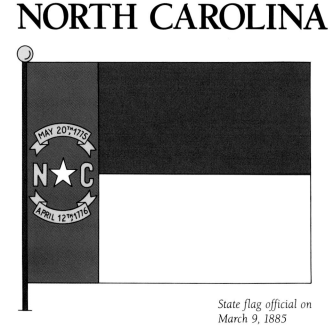

*State flag official on
March 9, 1885*

On May 20, 1861, the day North Carolina resolved to secede from the Union, Colonel John D. Whitford introduced a state flag ordinance. It stated that the "flag of this state shall be a blue **field** with a white V thereon, and a star, encircling which shall be the words: *Surgit astrum* ["We rise to the stars"], *May 20th, 1775*."

William G. Browne, an artist from Raleigh, submitted a model, but it differed from the original proposal. Browne's flag consisted of a red field with a white star in a semicircle. Browne used two dates. He placed May 20, 1861, the secession date, below the star and May 20, 1775, above the star.

May 20, 1775, represented the date of the Mecklenburg Declaration of Independence. The citizens of Mecklenburg County supposedly met to declare the county's independence from Great Britain. Although there is no written record that the meeting took place, North Carolina recognizes the Mecklenburg Declaration.

Browne's design was presented and accepted, and the troops of North Carolina regiments carried it throughout the Civil War.

After the Civil War, in 1885, the North Carolina legislature adopted a new state flag. General Johnstone Jones introduced a bill proposing a new design. The bill was passed on February 5, 1885. The flag now has one solid blue vertical bar with a white star in the center. The letter N is on one side of the star and the letter C is on the other. Both letters are in gilt (gold). The star and letters are bordered at the top and bottom by two scrolls bearing dates. The date of May 20, 1775, remains unchanged, but the 1861 date was replaced with April 12, 1776. This date commemorates the adoption of the Halifax Resolves, which stated that "the delegates for this Colony in the Continental Congress be empowered to concur with the delegates of the other colonies in declaring Independence...." The document stands out as one of the great events in North Carolina history.

The remainder of the flag is divided into two equally proportioned horizontal bars. The upper bar is red and the lower bar is white. The flag has remained unchanged since its adoption.

NORTH DAKOTA

State flag official on
March 3, 1911

The official flag of North Dakota is not well known to the people of the state and is displayed on comparatively few occasions. But North Dakotans can be very proud of the history of their flag.

The flag was carried by the men of the First North Dakota Volunteers during the Spanish-American War in 1895. The state's regiment also carried the flag when it was in the Philippines in 1899.

In 1924, Adjutant General G. A. Frazer presented this same battle flag and staff to the State Historical Society of North Dakota for preservation. Because the men of the First North Dakota Infantry had been in 37 battles, the staff is marked with 37 silver bands. The original words, *First North Dakota Infantry,* have been replaced by an embroidered silk scroll reading *North Dakota.*

In 1911, a full description of the state flag was written into law and officially adopted. The flag has a **field** of blue with a border of yellow fringe 2.5 inches (6.35 mm) wide. An eagle is **charged** in the center.

The figure of the bald eagle used on the North Dakota flag differs from the eagle on the official seal of the United States. The eagle on the national seal grasps thirteen arrows; the North Dakota eagle holds seven. The state's eagle grasps an olive branch with 3 red berries, while the national eagle bears an olive branch with 13 green olives. The national eagle's beak is clamped tightly, holding a scroll; the North Dakota eagle's beak is open with a scroll. And on the North Dakota flag, the shape of the shield on the eagle's breast is different.

The stars on the North Dakota seal also differ from the stars on the U.S. seal. On the U.S. seal, 13 stars are arranged in a large, six-pointed star and are surrounded by clouds. In the state flag of North Dakota, these stars are in two curved parallel rows surmounted by a gold sunburst.

To determine the proper color for the field of the state flag, a small piece of the original cloth was salvaged from the inside of the pole hem. This piece of cloth had been protected from the sun and the elements and clearly showed the original color, a deep violet blue, officially designated as cyanine blue.

The state was named after the Dakota tribe. *Dakota* means "allies" or "friends." North Dakota entered the Union, along with its sister state, South Dakota, on November 2, 1889. They were entered in alphabetical order as the 39th and 40th states.

OHIO

*State flag official on
May 9, 1902*

A new star was added to the Stars and Stripes in 1803 when Ohio was admitted to the Union as the 17th state. But it was not until 1901 that John Eisenmann, an architect and engineer, designed a flag for this new state.

The flag of Ohio has the distinction of being the only one of the 50 state flags designed as a **swallow-tailed** flag rather than as a traditional rectangle. Eisenmann's design called for a swallow-tailed flag of red, white, and blue.

The triangle formed by the main lines of the flag represents the hills and valleys of the state. The flag's stripes represent Ohio's roads and waterways. The stars, which indicate the 13 original states of the Union, are placed around a circle. Eisenmann added four more stars to show that Ohio was the 17th state to enter the Union.

The circle represents the Northwest Territory, from which Ohio was formed. The white circle around the red center represents the initial letter

O for Ohio and the fruit of Ohio's most famous tree, the buckeye. Ohio is nicknamed the "Buckeye State."

The flag of Ohio was shown for the first time in Buffalo, New York, at the Pan American Exposition of 1901. Officially, the "pennant" became the state flag on May 9, 1902.

Seven U.S. presidents were born in the state of Ohio. They were Ulysses S. Grant, Rutherford B. Hayes, James A. Garfield, Benjamin Harrison, William McKinley, William Howard Taft, and Warren G. Harding.

Other famous people who were born in Ohio include Neil Armstrong, the first person to walk on the moon; John Glenn, the first American to orbit the earth; and Thomas Edison, the inventor of the electric light and hundreds of other inventions.

Ohio's name comes from an Iroquois word meaning "something great." It was the first state to be carved from the area known as the Northwest Territory. Today it is a leading industrial state. Its motto is *With God, All Things Are Possible.*

OKLAHOMA

State flag official on
May 9, 1941

A total of 14 flags have been associated with Oklahoma. The first was the royal standard of Spain. That flag may have been brought to Oklahoma, or what now comprises the state of Oklahoma, by the Spanish explorer Francisco Vasquez de Coronado in 1541.

The second flag represented Great Britain. In 1663, King Charles II gave a wide strip of the New World, from the Atlantic to the Pacific, to his friends. This wide strip was known as Carolina and included nearly all of Oklahoma.

The third flag was French, planted in Oklahoma in 1719, although French claims date from the time of La Salle in 1682.

The fourth flag was the standard of the Spanish Empire because, in 1763, the French gave all the country west of the Mississippi to Spain in the Treaty of Paris. In 1800, Napoleon forced Spain to return the entire Louisiana Territory to France. Thus, the fifth flag was again French.

The sixth flag was that of the United States. France sold the Louisiana Territory to the United States in 1803. At the time, the United States flag had 15 stars and 15 alternating red and white stripes to represent the 15 states of the Union.

Even after it was purchased by the U.S., several other flags flew over Oklahoma before the Stars and Stripes returned. The flags of Mexico, the Republic of Texas, the Choctaw Indians, and the Confederacy appeared between 1821 and 1864. Oklahoma adopted its first state flag in 1911. This flag featured a red **field, charged** with a five-pointed, white star bordered with blue. The figure 46 designated Oklahoma as the 46th state to enter the Union.

The current flag, the 14th to fly over Oklahoma, was adopted in 1925, and the state name was added in 1941. The flag shows a sky-blue field. In the center is a Native American war shield of tan buckskin. Small crosses (the Native American design for stars) appear on the face of the shield, and seven eagle feathers hang from its edge. Crossing the shield are an olive branch and an ornamented calumet, or peace pipe, with a tassel at the end of the stem.

OREGON

State flag official on
February 26, 1925

Several persons and organizations are responsible for the state flag of
Oregon. In particular, Postmaster J. M. Jones of Portland wanted to see his
state represented in a display of state flags in the Post Office Building in
Washington, D.C. Senators Milton R. Klepper and J. O. Bailey introduced a
bill to request a design suitable for a state flag.

The official flag of Oregon was adopted in 1925. It bears the same shield
that forms the major part of the state's seal, which was designed by Harvey
Gordon in 1857. The flag is blue. In the center is a shield surrounded by
33 stars. The stars indicate that Oregon was the 33rd state to enter the
Union.

Pictured on the seal is an ocean scene showing a British warship departing
and an American steamer arriving. The scene depicts the change of control
over the Oregon Territory. Both England and the United States had occupied

the area, but in 1846, President James K. Polk signed a treaty with England, which gave the land to the United States.

The mountain, with an elk standing on a rocky ledge, represents the many mountain peaks and game herds found in the state. The covered wagon, the pioneers' major form of transportation, symbolizes the settling of the region. Authorities estimate that between 1839 and 1869, as many as 350,000 people followed the Oregon Trail to settle there.

The inscription, *The Union,* directly below the covered wagon, indicates Oregon's loyalty during the Civil War. The sheaf of wheat is symbolic of large agricultural yields. The plow symbolizes the industry of the farmer and the pickax is a tribute to the state's mining industry.

Perched above the shield, an eagle with widespread wings seems to be enfolding Oregon in the protection of the United States. The words *State of Oregon* appear across the upper portion of the flag, and the year of statehood, *1859,* appears on the lower portion.

The reverse side of the flag commemorates the state's nickname, the "Beaver State," with a beaver in gold on a navy blue **field.**

The first two flags were prepared on special order by a Portland retail store. The first was presented to the governor before being sent to Lexington, Massachusetts, for the 150th anniversary of the first battle of the Revolutionary War. The second went to Postmaster Jones, who donated his flag for the flag display at the Post Office Building in Washington, D.C.

PENNSYLVANIA

State flag official on
June 13, 1907

Pennsylvania was one of the 13 original colonies, but the official state flag was not described by law until June 13, 1907.

The flag's history can be traced through resolutions and acts of the general assembly. The Pennsylvania coat of **arms** first appeared on paper money issued by the state in 1777. By an act of April 9, 1799, provision was made for a state flag bearing the arms of the commonwealth. During the Civil War, many regimental flags were made by substituting the arms of Pennsylvania for the field of stars in the flag of the United States.

In 1878, Caleb Lowes of Philadelphia designed a new coat of arms with a shield, **crest**, supporters, and motto. The shield is composed of three parts: a plow, a ship under full sail, and three sheaves of wheat. The crest consists of an eagle with outstretched wings. Two black horses support the shield. The harnessed horses are rearing and facing each other. Below the shield is a cornstalk crossed by an olive branch. Extended below the base of the coat of arms is a ribbon with the state motto, *"Virtue Liberty and Independence."*

Not everyone was satisfied with Lowes's design, however. Certain elements, especially the horses, were unofficially changed from time to time. In 1809, one of the black horses appeared as a white horse. In 1823, the horses were pictured lying down. In 1829, one horse was left standing while the other horse reclined. By 1832, both horses were standing, but they were both white instead of the original black, and both were shown facing the same direction.

Pennsylvanians continued to make minor changes in the horses on their coat of arms until 1874, when official action became necessary. They wanted to exhibit the coat of arms during the centennial celebration of the independence of the United States. The celebration was to be held in Philadelphia in 1876, and Pennsylvania needed one official design for the occasion.

After discussing the situation, the general assembly appointed a commission to resolve the design problem. The commission submitted a report, and in 1875, the assembly voted to have two black chargers in the arms. The horses were to be fitted with a harness "by means of which they are ever prepared to draw the splendid car of state out of all difficulties on to the solid rock of ceaseless prosperity and perpetual affluence."

The design for the official state flag of Pennsylvania was approved on June 13, 1907. The design called for a solid blue **field** with the coat of arms of the commonwealth of Pennsylvania, embroidered in silk, in the center. The edge of the banner is trimmed with knotted yellow fringe, 2.5 inches (6.35 mm) wide. A cord of white and blue silk strands is attached to the staff at the spearhead.

RHODE ISLAND

*State flag official on
May 19, 1897*

In 1636, Roger Williams founded Rhode Island's first European settlement at Providence. Soon, three other settlements were established at Warwick, Portsmouth, and Newport.

In 1647, the four original towns united under one charter, held their first general assembly, and adopted the anchor as the official provincial seal. In 1664, the word *Hope* and a cable were added to the seal. The first known use of this seal appears on a document issued by the state general assembly, taking possession of a recently discovered gold mine, on November 10, 1648.

No formal action was taken in regard to a state flag until 1877. On March 30 of that year, the general assembly decided that the "flag of the state shall be a foul [tangled in a rope] anchor with the motto *Hope*; the whole to be surrounded by a scroll, around which, in a circle, shall be as many stars as there are states in the Union. The color of the anchor, motto, and stars, shall be blue, the scroll red in the center of a white **field**."

However, the only time the color red actually appeared on the state flag was during the years 1877 to 1882. The field remained white until February 1, 1882, when a new state flag was designed. By general consent, the design included a gold anchor surrounded by 13 gold stars on a blue field and the word *Hope* as the motto. No mention of the rope or cable was made.

Blue continued to be the color of the flag until Governor Charles W. Lippitt addressed the general assembly in 1897. He said, "In general orders detailed by Army Headquarters, New Winsor, New York, October 2, 1770, General Washington prescribed dark blue as the standard color of the uniform of the Continental Line of the Revolution and that the facings of New Hampshire, Massachusetts, Rhode Island, and Connecticut regiments should be white. On February 20, 1780, the Continental Board of War in Philadelphia, Pennsylvania, issued regulations prescribing that every regiment of the respective state lines should have two flags, one of the United States, the other that state, the ground whereof to be the color of the facing."

White once again became the authorized color for the field of the Rhode Island flag. The anchor is now gold. Free of the tangled rope, it stands above a blue scroll inscribed with the word *Hope*. The anchor is surrounded by 13 gold stars, representing the 13 original colonies, of which Rhode Island was one. The flag is edged with yellow fringe on three sides. Although it cannot be verified, the present state flag was probably designed by Judge G. M. Carpenter.

On May 19, 1897, the general assembly passed an act making the state flag official.

SOUTH CAROLINA

State flag official on
January 28, 1861

During the Revolutionary War, two South Carolina regiments were formed. Their uniforms were blue and their caps had silver crescents on them with the inscription "Liberty or Death." In September 1775, Fort Johnson, a British fort, was taken by these two regiments. Colonel William Moultrie, the commanding officer, wanted a flag to fly over the fort. He designed a large blue flag with a white crescent in the upper corner nearest the flagpole. The design complemented the troops' uniforms.

On June 28, 1776, the British fleet, under Sir Peter Parker, bombarded a fort (then unnamed) on Sullivan's Island. During the heated battle, the blue crescent flag was shot down. An enlisted man from the Second Regiment of the regular troops of South Carolina, Sergeant William Jasper, leaped over the wall of the fort and rescued the fallen flag.

Jasper placed the flag on the wall nearest the enemy. He gave three shouts before returning to his gallant company. The men continued to fight under Moultrie's command, and they inflicted great damage on the English fleet. The fort was named Fort Moultrie in honor of its commander and his stalwart defense.

The blue flag with the white crescent played an important role in the early history of South Carolina, but the palmetto tree was also important. The fort, built with sturdy logs from the palmetto tree, shielded the men from bombardment. Because of this, a white palmetto was added to the flag. It was **charged** in the center of the blue **field.**

About the time of the Civil War, vigorous attempts were made to change the state flag. Studies show that there were 19 recorded suggestions for color changes. Ideas for the flag's design ranged from a green palmetto tree to solid fields of various colors. But in 1861, the state assembly agreed to return to the original design and color—a blue field, a white crescent, and a white palmetto tree. It has remained unchanged since then.

SOUTH DAKOTA

*State flag official on
July 1, 1992*

The Dakota Territory was created in 1861. It took its name from the Sioux, who called themselves *Dakota,* meaning "allies" or "friends." South Dakota was admitted to the Union (with North Dakota) in 1889.

The state flag of South Dakota was a direct result of a request made by Seth Bullock to state Senator Ernest May of Deadwood. Captain Bullock had helped raise a troop of Dakota cowboys to take part in the Spanish-American War. They were members of the Third U.S. Volunteer Cavalry, better known as "the Rough Riders," who had charged San Juan Hill under Colonel Teddy Roosevelt. When Captain Bullock returned from service, he thought that there should be a state flag, and in 1908 he presented a request for one.

Senator May took immediate action. He asked State Historian Doane Robinson for a design. Robinson, in turn, called upon his secretary, Ida Anding McNeil of Pierre, South Dakota.

McNeil's design consisted of a **field** of blue in the center of which was a gold sun. In an arc above the sun, in gold letters, were the words *South Dakota,* and in an arc below the sun were the words *The Sunshine State,* also in gold letters.

Senator May introduced a bill to adopt the design, but the state senate amended the bill. The senate design placed the state seal on the reverse side. This flag became official on July 1, 1909.

The idea for the state seal came from Joseph Ward of Yankton. An artist illustrated Ward's idea, and the seal was presented and adopted in 1889. It was similar to, but not the same as, a seal adopted in 1885.

The seal depicts the lives of South Dakota settlers. The plowman symbolizes farming, and the cattle and grain represent ranching and dairying. The river and boat stand for transportation and commerce. The sawmill represents lumbering and manufacturing, while the smelting furnace symbolizes the mining industry. A scroll at the top of the scene reads *Under God the People Rule.* The entire scene is surrounded by a border bearing the words *Great Seal, State of South Dakota* and the year of statehood, *1889.*

By 1963 it became evident that a two-sided flag was too costly to produce. Legislation introduced by Representative William Sahr of Hughes County was enacted so that "all state flags made prior to effective date of this act shall remain official state flags, but the creation of a state flag from after the effective date of this act, other than in conformity herewith, is prohibited." This is from House Bill No. 503, signed into law March 11, 1963.

The flag now has rays, representing the sun, surrounding the state seal. In 1992 the words appearing around the sun's rays were changed from *South Dakota, The Sunshine State* to *South Dakota, The Mount Rushmore State.* This was done to honor the state's most popular tourist attraction.

TENNESSEE

*State flag official on
April 17, 1905*

Originally a part of North Carolina, Tennessee was settled by colonists from that state as well as from Virginia. In 1796, however, Tennessee was admitted into the Union as a separate state.

During the early days of the Civil War, a heated argument arose among the citizens of Tennessee. One group wanted to secede, and another wanted to remain in the Union. Finally, the state voted to secede. During the war, Tennessee was the site of many important battles, including the Battle of Lookout Mountain, which was fought on November 24, 1863. The victory of the Union forces at Nashville in 1864 gave the North control of the state. Following the Civil War, Tennessee was the first Confederate state to be readmitted into the Union, in 1866.

A state flag was adopted in 1897 for the Tennessee Centennial Exposition, but it wasn't often used. That flag bore the number *16*, indicating that

Tennessee was the 16th state to join the Union. It also had the nickname *The Volunteer State* written in yellow or gold letters. The nickname was gained because of Tennessee's outstanding reputation in furnishing troops to the armed forces.

It wasn't until 1905 that the state legislature adopted the present state flag, designed by Captain LeRoy Reeves of the Tennessee National Guard. The current design is a crimson **field** with a narrow white bar and a wider blue bar at the **fly** or outer end. The center of the field is **charged** with a blue circle in which there are three white stars. Around the edge of the circle is a white band. The three stars represent geographical regions which divide the state into three vertical parts: the Appalachian and Blue Ridge areas to the east, the Nashville Basin and Highland Rim in the center, and the Gulf Coastal Plain to the west. It has also been suggested that the stars represent the three presidents from Tennessee: Andrew Jackson, James Polk, and Andrew Johnson.

Reeves gave the following explanation of his design:

> The three stars are of pure white, representing the three grand divisions of the state. They are bound together by the endless circle of the blue field, the symbol being three bound together in one—an indissoluble trinity. The large field is crimson. The final blue bar relieves the sameness of the crimson field and prevents the flag from showing too much crimson when hanging limp. The white edgings contrast more strongly the other colors.

TEXAS

State flag official on
January 25, 1839

The flags of six different governments—Spain, France, Mexico, the Republic of Texas, the Confederate States, and the United States—have been raised over Texas, but there have also been many other flags.

During the 16th century, Spanish explorers claimed the territory for Spain, and the Spanish settled in the area that is now Texas.

In 1685, René-Robert Cavelier, Sieur de la Salle claimed the area for France. However, La Salle's colony was destroyed by Native Americans.

In 1803, President Thomas Jefferson purchased the Louisiana Territory from France. The territory included only a small part of Texas, but on the basis of earlier French claims, the United States claimed all territory as far south as the Rio Grande. In 1819, a treaty fixed the boundaries at the Sabine and Red rivers. This made the area that is now Texas part of Mexico.

Mexico broke away from Spain in 1821 and became a republic in 1824. Settlers living in the territory were under Mexican rule, but many of them were not happy with the policies of the Mexican president, General Santa Anna. Many of them wanted independence.

On December 11, 1835, they declared the town of San Antonio, Texas, to be free and independent. Before long, General Santa Anna arrived at the city with a large army and reclaimed the city for Mexico.

The Texas rebels withdrew behind the walls of an old Spanish mission called the Alamo. The Mexican forces attacked the Alamo, and on March 6, 1836, it fell. Among the brave men who lost their lives were Davy Crockett and Jim Bowie.

In an attempt to crush the revolution, Santa Anna ordered more than 330 people shot to death. But other Texans continued to fight. Under the command of Sam Houston, the Texans took the Mexican army by surprise and captured General Santa Anna. The victory ended the war, and the Texans gained independence. The Mexican flag came down.

The first official flag of the Republic of Texas, David G. Burnet's flag, was adopted on December 10, 1836. It was "of azure ground with a large golden star central."

But many other flags were displayed during the Texas revolution against Mexico. The flags were symbolic of the short-lived independence movements. One such flag was a red and white flag with a lone white star and the words, *Independence, Freedom, and Justice.* Another banner read *Come and Take It.* These words were painted on a white cotton cloth about six feet long. Above the words was an old cannon painted in black. Above the cannon was a lone star.

To stop the confusion, a committee was appointed in 1838 to design a flag. Law provided that the flag would officially consist of a blue perpendicular stripe, the width of one-third of the length of the flag. A white, five-pointed star is in the center of the blue stripe. Two horizontal stripes of equal breadth are to the right of the blue stripe. The upper stripe is white, and the lower stripe is red.

In 1845, when Texas became the 28th state, the Lone Star Flag became the state banner. But during the Civil War the Confederate flag was raised as the sixth flag to fly over Texas. With the end of the Civil War, the Stars and Stripes was hoisted once again and the Lone Star was reestablished as the state flag.

UTAH

State flag official on
March 11, 1913

In 1903, Utah's first flag was made from silk fiber produced by native silk worms that were raised in the homes of local pioneer women. The banner was woven by hand on Utah looms, and its brilliant blue dye was a product of native plants. The embroidery was stitched by patriotic women who followed the pattern of the state seal of Utah, which was designed by Utah artist Harry Edwards. The seal had been adopted by the legislature on April 3, 1896.

The Utah state flag is a symbol of the state's people, growth, and development. The Utah pioneers had very few tools when they came to the region, which they called *Deseret*, the Mormon word for "honeybee." The pioneers were ambitious, however, and the beehive, which stands for industry or hard work, symbolizes this. It is at the very center of the seal.

The sego lily pictured on each side of the beehive is an emblem of peace. It was sacred to the Native Americans in the region. The settlers ate the roots of the flower to stay alive after their provisions ran out, as did the Native Americans before them.

The word *Industry* above the beehive and the word *Utah* below it indicate the heritage the pioneers have passed on, a productive land won through hard work and determination.

The date *1847* appears on the seal to signify the date that the Mormons, who were seeking religious freedom under the leadership of Brigham Young, migrated to the territory. The Mormon settlement requested statehood but was refused by Congress because the Mormons practiced polygyny (the practice of being married to more than one wife at a time). This conflict between Utah and the government of the United States lasted from 1857 until 1890, when the Mormon church ordered the end of polygyny. Utah became a state in 1896, and this date appears on the bottom of the state seal.

A national flag flanks each side of the seal to express the patriotism of Utah citizens. The bald eagle, the emblem of the Union, rests atop the shield. The eagle's wings are outstretched as a symbol of protection. A gold fringe surrounds the flag on three sides. The first Utah state flag is still preserved in the state archives.

The second flag, created through the sponsorship of the Sons and Daughters of Utah Pioneers, was prepared by an Eastern firm for presentation to the battleship *Utah* in 1912. When the flag arrived, a gold ring had been added to the design. Although this was not a part of the original flag, many felt it added to the beauty of the flag, so it remained. Utah is proud of its history, and the present state flag symbolizes that pride. The design of the flag became official on March 11, 1913.

Different organizations have appealed over the years to change the complicated design of the state flag, but all have failed in their efforts.

VERMONT

State flag official on
March 26, 1923

In 1609, Samuel de Champlain was probably the first white person to explore the area that is now Vermont. He arrived at Lake Champlain and claimed the area for France. The word *Vermont* is derived from the French words *vert mont*, meaning "green mountain." Vermont's nickname is the "Green Mountain State." Vermont was admitted to the Union as the 14th state in 1791.

In 1803, a state flag was adopted. In keeping with the original design of the national flag, the Vermont flag had 17 alternating red and white stripes and 17 white stars on a blue **field.** (The additional stars and stripes represented Kentucky, Tennessee, and Ohio.) The flag also showed the word *Vermont* in capital letters. Putting the name of the state on it made the new flag distinctive.

On October 20, 1837, the Vermont legislature redesigned the state flag so it had 13 red and white stripes. One large white star, representing the Union, and the state's coat of **arms** were **charged** on a blue field. Although the design for this flag was approved by the legislature, there is little evidence that it was used or displayed. In fact, in 1923, when the question of changing the flag was brought up again, legislators found that there were only a few of these flags in existence and that very few people were familiar with the design.

Vermont's present flag, designed by Robert Temple, consists of a field of solid blue with the state coat of arms charged in the center. A green landscape occupies half the shield. In the background, blue mountains rise beneath a yellow sky. Reaching almost from the base to the top of the shield is a green pine tree. To the left of the tree are three sheaves of grain. A red cow stands to the right of the tree. The scene depicts the agricultural, dairy, and lumber industries, as well as the marble and granite quarries found in the state. A scroll beneath the shield bears the motto *Vermont, Freedom and Unity*. Two pine branches form a half wreath around the lower half of the shield, and a buck's head, symbolizing the state's wildlife, is at the top of the shield.

VIRGINIA

State flag official on
April 30, 1861

Virginia was the first part of the country to be settled by English colonists, early in the 17th century. In 1584, Sir Walter Raleigh and Queen Elizabeth named the colony Virginia.

The state flag proudly proclaims Virginia's love of freedom, which was demonstrated during the American Revolution against England. Virginia furnished four of the first five presidents of the United States. During the Civil War, the state split. The western section remained loyal to the Union and became a separate state under the name of West Virginia.

Virginia adopted its state flag on April 30, 1861, and has used this flag ever since. (More precise forms were designated in 1931 and 1949.) The flag has a deep blue **field** with a circular white center of the same material. Upon this circle, on both sides of the flag, Virginia's seal is painted or embroidered, as described in section 27 of the Code of Virginia. The flag is fringed in white on the **fly** end, the end farthest from the flagpole.

The state seal that is **charged** in the center of the flag was designed by some of the greatest minds of the day. Chosen from among prominent leaders of the Continental Congress, the design committee consisted of Richard Henry Lee, George Mason, Robert Carter Nicholas, and George Wythe. Exact authorship of the design remains a disputed point among historians, but Whitney Smith, a recognized leader in the field of **vexillology** (study of flags), credits only George Wythe.

Pictured on the seal is Virtue, the symbol of the commonwealth. She is dressed like an Amazon, a female warrior. Virtue holds a spear with one hand and a sword in the other. She treads on Tyranny, represented by a man completely overcome, his crown fallen from his head. He holds a broken chain in his left hand and a whip in his right hand. The phrase that appears at the base of the seal, *Sic Semper Tyrannis* means "Thus Always to Tyrants."

Because variations of the design began to appear, the general assembly passed an act in 1873, and again in 1903, describing the seal in great detail. The seal, as it appears on the state flag, is correct in all major details.

WASHINGTON

State flag official on
June 7, 1923

No foreign flag has ever flown over the soil of Washington, although the area was visited and claimed by Spanish and British explorers in the 1780s. Captain Robert Gray reached the area in 1792. Based on his arrival at the Columbia River, the United States also claimed the region. The expedition led by Lewis and Clark in 1805 gave the United States a second claim, but both British and American fur traders continued to operate in the area during the early 1800s.

The War of 1812 greatly hampered development of the territory, as both British and American fur traders suffered severe losses during the conflict. The war was followed by a period of growth, and many people settled in "Oregon Country," as the region was called during the 1840s. Lumbering and mining were two major attractions. Soon the plains farmers followed the miners and the lumberjacks, and small communities began to sprout.

The completion of a railroad connection with the East brought more settlers in the 1880s, and the shipping industry thrived and added wealth to the railroads.

Although an effort to secure statehood was made as early as 1878, when a constitution was drafted and adopted by the voters, their efforts failed when Congress turned down their claim for statehood. Eleven years later, the people of Washington appealed again to Congress. This time they were successful, and on November 11, 1889, their star was added to the flag of the United States as the 42nd state to enter the Union.

In 1914, the national headquarters of the Daughters of the American Revolution asked the Washington chapter for a state flag to hang in Memorial Continental Hall in Washington, D.C. A committee, headed by Charles Miles, was appointed to look into the matter. The committee checked at Olympia, the state's capital, and found no state flag existed.

The committee designed a flag, which was submitted to the state assembly of the Daughters of the American Revolution in 1915. It was a solid green banner, representing the "Evergreen State," and in the center was **charged** the state seal, which bears a picture of George Washington's head. The design was endorsed by the assembly.

When they reached Washington, D.C., the ladies of the assembly had a state banner made from the design and presented it to Memorial Continental Hall. The banner was of rich green silk with the bust of George Washington in the center. It is the only flag of the 50 states with a green **field.**

In 1916 the flag made its first appearance in the state. On loan from Continental Hall, it hung over the speaker's desk at the 15th DAR assembly, over which Mrs. Edmund Bowden of Seattle presided. The DAR continued to campaign for a state flag and, in 1923, the state legislature officially adopted the banner. According to state law, "the edges of the flag may, or may not, be fringed. If a fringe is used the same shall be of gold or yellow color…."

WEST VIRGINIA

State flag official on
March 7, 1929

The origin of West Virginia's state flag is very different from that of other state flags. In fact, the story of West Virginia's statehood is unique. It was born during the days of the Civil War. West Virginia was a part of Virginia until 1861, when settlers in the western part of the state refused to fight against the Union. During the Union campaign, orders that all regiments must have banners were issued. The first state flag of West Virginia stemmed from those regimental flags.

In 1863, West Virginia's star was added to the flag of the United States. On January 28, 1864, it was resolved that:

> ...as an evidence of their appreciation of the heroism and valor of the officers and soldiers comprising the Fourth Regiment West Virginia Volunteer Infantry, in the battle(s) of Charleston, Vicksburg, Jackson and Mission Ridge, the governor is hereby authorized and requested to present to the said regiment, on behalf of the loyal citizens of this state, a flag adapted to their

arm of service with the coat of **arms** of this state and the following inscription placed legibly thereupon, viz:

Vicksburg, Miss. May 19th and 22nd, 1863

Jackson, Miss. July 9th and 12th, 1863

Mission Ridge November 25, 1863…

After that resolution, the other 25 West Virginia regiments also wanted flags. All the flags were six feet square and made of dark blue silk with a golden fringe. One side bore the state seal, the name of the regiment, their battles, and the dates of each battle. The other side was **charged** with the national coat of arms, an eagle with a shield protecting its breast, arrows in its right talon, and an olive branch in its left.

It was not until the Louisiana Purchase Exposition in 1904 that the need for one state flag became urgent. At the exposition, which was held in St. Louis, the West Virginia exhibit could not have 26 flags hoisted above it.

A commission recommended a design which had a white **field** with a sprig of the state flower, *rhododendron maximum* or "big laurel," bearing flowers and leaves, pictured in the center. On the reverse side was the state coat of arms and the motto *Montani Semper Liberi*, "Mountaineers Always Freemen."

This design was highly impractical because the lettering on one side read in mirror image (from right to left), and the colors on each side of the white field showed through to the opposite side. Unofficially, manufacturers began to redesign the state flag as early as 1913 so that it could be stamped from dies that would show both the seal and the flower on the same side.

In 1929, the state legislature adopted the present flag. In the center of a pure white field is the coat of arms, upon which appears the date of admission to the Union along with the state motto. The coat of arms shows a farmer and a miner flanking a rock. In the foreground is a pair of crossed hunters' rifles. A Phrygian cap (cap of liberty) rests on top of them at the point where they cross. Above the coat of arms there is a ribbon which reads *State of West Virginia*. Arranged appropriately around the lower part of the seal is a wreath of rhododendron, the state flower. The field of white is bordered by a strip of blue on all sides.

WISCONSIN

*State flag official on
May 1, 1981*

The original state flag of Wisconsin is over a century old. The flag was first designed in 1863. After the Civil War, however, the Wisconsin National Guard used a different flag, and, in 1887, the legislature mistakenly repealed the legal provisions for the state flag. But in April 1913, new legal action was taken. The state's banner was to be reduced from 6 feet 6 inches by 6 feet to 5 feet 6 inches by 4 feet 4 inches. It was to be a **field** of dark blue silk with the state coat of **arms** embroidered on each side in appropriate colors.

The coat of arms tells much of Wisconsin's history. Beneath the seal are a horn of plenty and a pyramid of lead bars, each representing wealth derived from the earth. The shield is divided into four sections and each section bears a symbol of the early pioneers and their contribution to the state's development: a plow for agriculture, an arm and hammer for manufacturing, a crossed shovel and pick for mining, and an anchor for navigation.

The shield is supported by a sailor holding a coil of rope and a miner holding a pick. The two represent labor on water and labor on land.

A badger rests above the shield. This strong, aggressive animal was chosen with deep affection to represent the state. *Badgers* was a name given to the Wisconsin lead miners, who poured into the state during the 1820s. Some of the miners lived in caves in the hillsides. Badgers dig holes in the ground in much the same way as the miners dug their caves. Wisconsin's nickname is the "Badger State."

The motto *Forward* is printed on a ribbon over the coat of arms. This motto was introduced in 1851 after Governor Nelson Dewey and Justice Edward Ryan revised the seal. Justice Ryan objected to the Latin motto *Excelsior* which had been proposed. As an alternative, Ryan suggested *Forward*.

In 1979, the state legislature revised the flag, and the revisions became effective in 1981. The word *Wisconsin,* in white capital letters, was added in the center above the coat of arms, and the date *1848*, in white, was added in the center below the coat of arms. In 1848, Wisconsin entered the Union as the 30th state. All new flags must conform to the new requirements, but flags manufactured before May 1, 1981, may still be used as state flags.

WYOMING

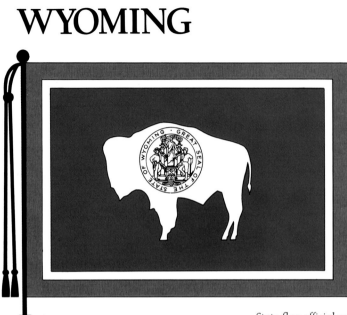

The Wyoming state flag was designed by Verna Keays of Buffalo, Wyoming, later to become Mrs. A. C. Keyes of Casper, Wyoming. The design was adopted in 1917. Its colors are red, white, and blue. A deep red border represents the Native Americans of the original territory. Tribes that were in the area include the Arapaho, Arikara, Bannock, Blackfeet, Crow, Cheyenne, Gros Ventre, Kiowa, Shoshoni, Sioux, and Ute. The red border also represents the blood shed by the pioneers and the Native Americans. White is the emblem of purity and honor. Blue is the color of the sky and the mountains. The blue in the flag is also symbolic of fidelity, justice, and virility or strength.

In the center of the blue **field** is a bison, once the king of the plains and a source of much-needed food and clothing for the pioneers and the Native Americans. In keeping with the custom of the open range, the buffalo on Wyoming's flag is branded, in this case with the state seal.

The two dates on the seal, *1869* and *1890,* mark the organization of territorial government and Wyoming's later admission to the Union. The number *44* signifies that Wyoming was the 44th state to be admitted to the Union. The draped figure in the center of the Wyoming seal is a symbol of the civil and political rights of women. Wyoming had the honor of being the first state to allow women to vote. The woman in the center of the seal is standing before a banner proclaiming equal rights. Two men support her, one a cattleman holding a lasso and dressed in range attire, and the other a miner holding a pick. The rancher represents cattle and grain, while the miner represents the minerals and oil hidden beneath the surface.

The name Wyoming was adopted from a Delaware word, *Mecheweami-ing.* To the Native Americans, the phrase meant "at the big flats" or "upon the great plain."

GLOSSARY

argent: the heraldic color silver or white

arms or coat of arms: a distinctive emblem which may consist of a shield, crest, motto, and supporters

bordure: the border surrounding a heraldic shield

canton: the upper corner of a flag next to the flagpole

charged: placed on a flag or shield; refers to a coat of arms or other emblem that is placed on a flag

colors: flags carried by military units or used by a military officer

crest: the part of a coat of arms that appears above the shield

dexter: a word that means right in heraldic terminology. This is from the point of view of someone standing *behind* the flag, not that of the viewer.

field: the background of a flag

fly: the part of the flag that is farthest from the flagpole. The term is also used for the length of an extended flag from its flagpole.

hoist: the part of the flag that is closest to the flagpole. The term is also used for the width of a flag.

obverse: the front of a flag or seal

rococo: an artistic style of the 18th century that is characterized by fanciful, curved forms and elaborate ornamentation

saltire: a diagonal cross

sinister: a word that means left in heraldic terminology. This is from the point of view of someone standing *behind* the flag, not that of the viewer.

swallow-tailed: a term applied to flags with a deeply forked or V-shaped cut in the fly

vexillologist: a person who studies flags

vexillology: the study of flags

Parts of a Flag

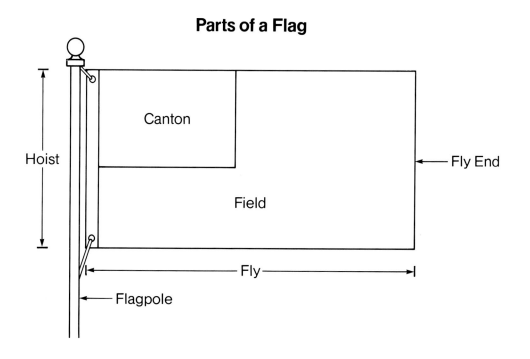